The Board Game Designer's Guide to Careers in the Industry

Are you thinking about working in the board game industry? Here's what you need to know.

There are so many jobs and roles that need to be filled in the board game industry. You might just have the right skills and experience to excel. But first, you need to know what opportunities exist and what the hardest gaps are to fill!

In this book, you'll discover:

- What jobs are really in demand
- How you can get your foot in the door with a publisher
- Jobs in the industry you've never even thought of
- What other opportunities exist for people with skills just like yours

With insights from over 40 industry pros, as well as the author's many years of experience, you'll be able to put your own skills and experience to great use in an amazing, growing industry.

T0386415

The Board Game Designer's Guide to Careers in the Industry

Joe Slack

CRC Press
Taylor & Francis Group
Boca Raton London New York

CRC Press is an imprint of the
Taylor & Francis Group, an **informa** business

First edition published 2023
by CRC Press
6000 Broken Sound Parkway NW, Suite 300, Boca Raton, FL 33487-2742

and by CRC Press
4 Park Square, Milton Park, Abingdon, Oxon, OX14 4RN

CRC Press is an imprint of Taylor & Francis Group, LLC

Library of Congress Cataloging-in-Publication Data

Names: Slack, Joe, author.
Title: The boardgame designer's guide to careers in the industry/Joe Slack.
Description: Boca Raton, FL: CRC Press, 2023. | Includes bibliographical references and index.
Identifiers: LCCN 2022024161 (print) | LCCN 2022024162 (ebook) | ISBN 9781032369044 (hardback) | ISBN 9781032368931 (paperback) | ISBN 9781003334408 (ebook)
Subjects: LCSH: Board game industry–Vocational guidance. | Board games–Design and construction.
Classification: LCC HD9993.G352 S53 2023 (print) | LCC HD9993.G352 (ebook) | DDC 794.023–dc23/eng/20220801
LC record available at https://lccn.loc.gov/2022024161
LC ebook record available at https://lccn.loc.gov/2022024162

ISBN: 978-1-032-36904-4 (hbk)
ISBN: 978-1-032-36893-1 (pbk)
ISBN: 978-1-003-33440-8 (ebk)

DOI: 10.1201/9781003334408

Typeset in Garamond
by KnowledgeWorks Global Ltd.

Contents

Section III
Freelancing

Section IV
Everything You Wanted to
Know about Other Roles
but were Too Afraid to Ask

Other Books by Joe Slack

The Board Game Designer's Guide
(https://tinyurl.com/boardgameguide)

The Board Game Designer's Guide to Getting
Published (https://routledge.com/9781032369884)

The Top 10 Mistakes New Board Game Designers Make (and How to Avoid Them) (https://tinyurl.com/top10gamedesign)

Praise for Joe's Other Books

"Without a doubt, if I had read Joe's book back in 1989, it would have accelerated my progress and potential as a game designer by decades."

–Jamey Stegmaier, Stonemaier Games (Scythe)

"My wife and I were very excited to be able to read and contribute to Joe's work - he's prolific in the Canadian community, and his insights have helped many figure out how to not only have their game successfully signed, but succeed in the journey. As a publisher, the book has been very insightful as well as the industry normalizes contracts and becomes more streamlined. Highly recommended for our ever-changing market!"

–Dan Kazmaier, Steeped Games (Chai)

"If you have a game idea and [are] wondering how to bring it to life - this book is your definitive first step."

–Artem Safarov, Altema Games (Unbroken)

"Slack's book is accessible and informative. Wish I had been able to read it years ago. If you are just starting out in trying to get published, this book boils down info that has taken me two years to learn on my own… the section interviewing publishers is like peeling back the curtain on OZ."

–Adam Michaud

"I have read most of the 'top' board game design books, and this one is up there with the best of them. It is a reference that I will be going back to time and time again as I develop my games."

–Chris Kingsnorth

"This is an essential resource for new designers and the pros may learn something as well. I highly recommend buying this book."

–Neal Rusch

"A big thumbs up for being an easy read, yet one that is packed with useful tips and tricks.… Buy it, you won't regret it."

–Stephanie D. Schultz

Check out Joe's helpful blogs, books, and courses at boardgamedesigncourse. com

Acknowledgements

First, I must thank Scott Gaeta, CEO of Renegade Games for his incredible presentation at Proto TO, which inspired me to write this book.

Second, I must thank all the amazing contributors who provided so many great stories and such helpful advice for others trying to get into the industry. This book wouldn't be nearly as valuable without all of your assistance.

Thank you Sebastian Koziner, Matt Paquette, Peter C. Hayward, Ori Kagan, Joe Aubrey, David Diaz, Alexander Schmidt, Fertessa Allyse, David Bloomberg, Hanna Björkman, Jeff Fraser, Sen-Foong Lim, Nalin Chuapetcharasopon, Dave Snyder, A.J. Brandon, Jon Homfray, Bernd Eisenstein, Brandon Rollins' Sydney Engelstein, Chris Cormier, Shero Li, Tristam Rossin, Jean-Baptiste Ramassamy, Jesse Samuel Anderson, Mark Maia, Cameron Art, Dustin Staats, Rachael Blaske, Charlie McCarron, Kathleen Mercury, Gabe Barrett, Jason Schneider, Joshua Lobkowicz, John Zinser, Adam McCrimmon, Jamey Stegmaier, Anne-Marie De Witt, Justin De Witt, Debbie Moynihan, Curt Covert, and Vincent Vergonjeanne.

Research also included contributions from Nikki Valens, Matt Holden, Kwanchai Moriya, Beth Sobel, Vincent Dutrait, Dustin Schwartz, Darren Watts, Kerry Rundle, Sarah Graybill, Katia Howatson, Mitch Morris, and Cristo Daniel.

To all the amazing game designers and community members I've learned from, and in many cases became friends with, over the years, I wouldn't be where I am without all of you. Thank you Sylvain Plante, Nazareno Properzi, Daryl Andrews, Jonathan Gilmour, Rob Daviau, Steve Jackson, Matt Leacock, Jay Cormier, Uwe Rosenberg, Kristian Amundsen Ostby, Wolfgang Warsch, Rudiger Dorn, Kane Klenko, Alan Moon, Bruno Cathala, Kevin Lanzing, JB Howell, Vlaada Chvatil, Tom Vasel, Luke Laurie, Eduardo Baraf, Colby Dauch, Ben Gerber, Gil Hova, Daniel Zayas, the late James Mathe, Artem Safarov, Mark Kolb, Pam Walls, Shannon

McDowell, Matthew Hester, Kevin Carmichael, Allysha Tulk, Daniel Rocchi, Jeff Fraser, Stephanie Metcalf, Marek Tupy, Harry Timson, David Van Drunen, David Laciak, Miles Bossons, Andy Kim, Shawn Clouthier, Sherri Cormier, Sean Calligan, Maryann Buri, Marc Gurwiz, Chris Backe, Graham MacLean, Mikhail Honoridez, Reed Mascola, Jack Kennedy, Al Leduc, Josh Derkson, Brian Stumme, Adam Springer, Francois Valentine, Josh Sprung, Caren Sprung, Kenny Valles, Scott Kelly, Bill Murphy, Erica Bouyouris, Grace Lee, Tristam Rossin, Corey Keller, Chad Crider, Michael Chartrand, Stephen Sauer, Danny Goodisman, Lutfi Nahin, Bryan Dale, Brent Wilde, David Clay Gonsalves, Darryl T Jones, Chris Medeiros, Jesse Anderson, Joel Colombo, Amelia Le-Roche, Patrick Hardy, Adam Leamey, Darrin Lauritzen, Colin Eatock, Jeff Toth, Timothy Metcalfe, Chris Zinsli, Richard MacRae, Julia Patrick, and the whole team at XYZ Game Labs.

A huge thank you to Qat Wanders and Christina Bagni from Wandering Words Media for their incredible editing skills, which made this book so much better!

Thank you as well to Drew Corkill for the amazing book cover and formatting.

To my incredible friends and family, Jason Deline, Helena Patte, Matthew Guillemette, the late Margie Guillemette, Aizick Grimann, Lubin Martinez, Lucas Cesarone, Daniel Longmire, Dave Neal, Renee Laviolette, Claudia Mendez, Matt Mitchell, Cory Bildfell, Rob Slack, Kerri Beaulieu, Sawyer Slack, Kenya Slack, Penny Slack, John Acuna, Cindy Alexander, Caitlin Hartley, Jordan Loshinsky, Melissa McCarthy, Kate McDougall, Stu Sackler, Siva Bradshaw, Shannon Boyce, Marco Garcia, Helen Deline, Gary Deline, Paul Brown, Nan Brooks, Jane Goldthorpe, Mike Sone, Adam DeVita, Frances Maxwell, Voula Maroulis, Jeremy Banks, Nathan Frias, Chad Nikolic, Margarita Prunskus, Pat Prunskus, Yvonne Tellis, James Pawelkiewicz, Leah Smith, Adam Smith, Momo MacLeod, Dave Rossi, Belinda Rossi, Krista Miller, Bernard Blassnig, Rob Routh, Kim Routh, Anna Murray, Helen Taylor, Steve Camacho, Andrew Gibson, Kelly Walk Hines, Lana Jo Borgholthaus, Mike Indovina, Jocelyn Phillips, Shannon Wylie, Kunle Bristow, Deb Piskunov, and Maks Piskunov. Thank you all for your support and for playing so many early prototypes of my games.

Thank you to my parents, Nancy and Bob Slack. Thank you for everything you do and for always being so supportive.

Last but not least, thank you, Lisa and Evan, for being there for me and letting me live my dream!

About the Author

Joe Slack is a healthcare data guru turned full-time board game designer and game design instructor. He has now combined his passions for board game design and helping others into one. That means he works with other board game designers to help them get unstuck and create amazing games they can't wait to share with the world.

Joe is the #1 best-selling author of *The Board Game Designer's Guide*, *The Board Game Designer's Guide to Getting Published*, and *The Top 10 Mistakes New Board Game Designers Make (and How to Avoid Them)*.

Joe has four games published with different publishers (*Zoo Year's Eve*, *Kingdom's Candy Monsters*, *Four Word Thinking*, and *King of Indecision*), along with one self-published game, the solo campaign game *Relics of Rajavihara*.

Joe has also taught game design and development at Wilfrid Laurier University (near Toronto, Canada), and currently runs two online game design courses (the Board Game Design Course and the Creation to Publication Program) that he developed himself, along with a membership site for game designers.

Please visit www.boardgamedesigncourse.com to check out his blog, resources, books, and courses made entirely for game designers. You can also see what games he's currently working on at www.crazylikeabox.com.

Introduction

It seems like every board gamer wants to be a game designer.

I get it. To make something awesome that thousands or even millions of people enjoy is an amazing creative pursuit.

But there are so many other roles in the board game industry besides "designer" that are often overlooked, or not nearly as well known.

Not every member of a rock band can be a charismatic lead singer. You need an amazing lead guitarist to play those blistering solos. You need a great rhythm section, delivering a funky bassline and thumping drums. You may also have a rhythm guitarist, keyboard player, and other members to round out the sound. Plus, some members contribute background vocals, write lyrics and music, and do a whole lot more. And that's not even taking into account all the non-musicians that make the band possible, like the marketers, producers, engineers, and managers. There are so many people behind the scenes that nobody will ever see.

Suffice it to say, the whole band is never just one person.

The same goes for a great board game. Many hands are involved in the process from that first idea until it arrives in the customer's hands.

This book was inspired by a talk by Scott Gaeta, CEO of Renegade Games, held at Proto TO, a local Toronto game design event a few years back. In the session, Scott talked about all the other important jobs in the industry besides game design, including some big gaps that need to be filled by people with the right mix of skills and experience.

Consider for a moment all the things that go into creating and publishing a game:

- Game design
- Playtesting
- Blind playtesting
- Development
- Rule writing
- Story writing (in some cases)

DOI: 10.1201/9781003334408-1

- Art
- Graphic design
- Promotion
- Marketing
- Reviews
- Product launch
- Publishing
- Manufacturing
- Shipping
- Fulfilment
- Sales
- Customer Service

The list goes on.

Sure, one person *could* do all (or at least most) of these things, but are they really going to be able to do every one of these tasks well? We all know the term "Jack of all trades, master of none." It is definitely important, as you'll see, to be good at (or learn to get good at) multiple things, but we also have to realize that having many experts (or masters) involved will result in a much better game than one "Jack" could ever produce.

That's why it's so important to recognize that there are so many critical roles in the industry that go way beyond game design.

In this book, you'll discover roles in the industry you didn't even know existed. Not only that, but you'll also learn what skills, experience, and education are necessary to land these jobs and start working in the board game industry.

You'll discover that many of the roles discussed in this book don't require a University degree or thirty years of experience. Most positions are self-taught. You can learn a lot on the job and develop those skills into invaluable traits that are sought after in the industry.

I'll cover everything from freelance game design and development to working in-house for a publisher (and all the many roles needed there). We'll even discuss manufacturing, shipping, retail, and so much more. There are so many opportunities, and soon you'll know exactly where you can fit in within this amazing industry.

I've reached out to over forty people in the industry, from publishers to rulebook writers to content creators to other ancillary businesses to find out how they landed their jobs, what helped them get there, and what roles they feel are really needed and are the hardest to fill. With this knowledge, you'll know exactly what gaps exist and how you can help to fill them, jumpstarting your career in the board game industry.

Here are some of the themes you'll see throughout this book:

The pay generally isn't great. People aren't in the board game industry to make a quick buck or strike it rich. They are in it because they love board games, enjoy the creativity and flexibility that often comes with the job, and value these things above money. If you're looking for easy money, this probably isn't the place for you.

You need to have good interpersonal skills. Board games, by nature, are highly social. Working in the industry is no different. You need to be able to communicate effectively and be able to listen to and work with others. You must be able to clearly articulate what you want out of a project, explain what you bring to a project, and understand what others want to get out of a project.

You need to be a good problem-solver. Whether you are developing a game, working as a publisher, are involved in shipping and fulfillment, providing art or graphic design services, creating content, or anything else, you constantly need to get to the root of an issue and find viable solutions. Game designers are constantly solving problems (and often adding new ones when we fix others), but this thread is common throughout the industry, not just in design.

You need to be motivated and have a great work ethic. It goes without saying that being a hard worker is important. You need to constantly be learning, improving, and getting better in your role. You need to be curious. And you need to be willing to put in the time and effort to build a portfolio, a reputation, and gain the trust of others. Many roles in the industry are freelance or otherwise fairly independent, and you need to be able to deliver results.

A lot can come down to who you know. Board games are a social activity, and so is the industry. It thrives on conventions and events that bring people together. So, it's in your best interest to network with lots of people in the industry, in person and/or online. Helping out a publisher by demoing games at a convention, reviewing a rulebook, or playtesting and providing great feedback can lead to something much bigger. A company is more likely to take a chance on you if they know and trust you rather than someone they've never met.

Big and small publishers run quite differently. While a large publisher might have a team of developers and specialists in many roles, a small publisher might only have two to five employees. There are many more small publishers than large ones and it can often be hard to justify hiring within an industry that is known for instability and small margins.

You'll have to wear many hats. While you'll likely be hired into a specific role based on the expertise you have shown, many publishers have few employees, so you'll be asked to take on, and get good at many things. If you're into growth and learning, there are tremendous opportunities to uncover all the behind-the-scenes aspects of the industry.

If this scares you, then I suggest you put this book down and walk away slowly.

But if you're just as excited now (or even more) as when you picked up this book to discover more about the critical jobs that need to be filled in the industry and how you can find your niche, keep reading and join us on this journey as we take a deeper look into how you can use your own experience, education, and skills to become a part of the board game industry.

Section I

Game Creation

1

Game Design

The first job that comes to most people's minds when they think about the board game industry is game designer. It is the highly romanticized creative role most people gravitate toward. They've played lots of different games and want to try creating one themselves.

That's why I've focused on game design for the first chapter of this book. But before we get started, I want to make it clear …

Game Design Is a Difficult Job

From the outside, being a game designer looks easy. You just come up with an idea and make a game about it. It's just as simple as that.

What people don't see, and what often makes many aspiring game designers quit pretty early on, is all the hard work, constant changes, criticism, and rejection you face on the long road to becoming a published game designer (if that is your end goal).

It's easy to make a game, but it's a challenge to make a truly great game. It's a whole lot harder than this to make a career out of making board games.

That's why the overwhelming majority of game designers do this on the side as a hobby or as a freelancer. I'd wager that less than 5 percent of all game designers do this as a full-time job. Even those who are full-time game designers often supplement their income in other ways, like teaching, doing game development, taking on other work, or consulting from outside the industry.

I quit my job over four years ago to do game design "full time," but still fully expected that I wouldn't be doing game design 100 percent of the time.

DOI: 10.1201/9781003334408-3

I've always loved helping and teaching others, so I knew that going into it I would also continue to write more books on game design (my first one came out well before I transitioned to game design as a career; this book is my fourth), teach game design through my own private courses (I also had a stint teaching game design and development at Laurier University), and do other things to help game designers, such as running the Board Game Design Virtual Summit and writing helpful weekly blogs on game design.

Many who want to become professional game designers quickly find out that it's hard to support themselves (let alone a family) when their income fluctuates so much. You might get an advance on a game you signed (if you're fortunate), but then it could easily be a year or two (or more) before you start to see any royalties for this game roll in.

Even if you have multiple games published, the payouts you receive will be erratic. I've received a payment of $1,245 for one game and then waited a full twelve months before receiving any other royalty payments. Most games also don't have a very long tail. By that, I mean that most sales happen when a game is first released (especially if it goes through Kickstarter), then sales decline and the game doesn't sell nearly as well even a few months after this.

Unless your game becomes the next *Ticket to Ride* or *Catan* (and these evergreen hits are few and far between), it's going to be very challenging to make a decent living by designing games alone.

That's why many who attempt to make game design a full-time career often end up branching out into other areas, such as graphic design, rulebook writing and editing, or starting their own publishing company. I've seen many aspiring designers find enough work in these other roles to turn them into full-time jobs. They then often have to push game design to the backburner and have this as more of a side hobby, much as they did when they were first starting to design their own games while working full time in another industry.

If you have the right skillset, experience, and connections, you'll be much more in demand as a rulebook writer or game developer than a game designer.

We'll get into all these options, plus a whole lot more, throughout this book.

However, if you're still thinking of designing games for a living (or even as a part-time gig), let's talk about what options are available to you.

Working for a Publisher

Most publishers are fairly small. They might even be a one-man or one-woman show. That often means that this individual does everything from designing to publishing their own games.

Others only have a small number of employees, and a full-time game designer is not likely to be one of them. It's much more likely that they will license games from freelance game designers (more on this in a moment) or only publish games the owner has designed. It's not likely they will be hiring anyone for the role of game designer anytime soon.

Only a small number of the larger publishers will even have the role of a game designer on their team. Even in these cases, you're looking at really large companies that are often in both the toy and board game world, like Hasbro and Mattel, who produce more mass market, toy-like games for younger audiences. So, if you're into designing heavy Euros along the lines of *Terraforming Mars* and *Puerto Rico*, this may not be the right fit for you.

Even if you are able to land a job with a publisher, keep in mind that you might not be able to work on your own independent games. At least, not with the intention of publishing them. Depending on what your contract says, any games you create will likely become the property of the publisher you are working for, so, be aware of these possible limitations.

It's far more likely you'll work as an independent freelance game designer if you attempt to make a career out of creating games, so let's dive into this option further.

Working as a Freelance Game Designer

Designing games for a living is equal parts exciting and scary.

One of the biggest benefits of working freelance as a game designer is freedom. Freedom to create the games you want to make. Freedom to choose which publishers you work with (if they also choose you!). Freedom to spend your time as you wish and work wherever you choose.

It's amazing when you've created something that many people can get joy from, and even more amazing when you find a publisher that understands your vision and wants to bring your idea to life. At the same time, you have no idea whether the game will sell ten copies or ten thousand copies.

Sure, you've made a great game and done everything you can to deliver an amazing experience for players, but everything else is up to the publisher. They have to convey what makes your game so special to others and market it well enough to sell out the first print run or execute a successful Kickstarter campaign.

You are likely going to earn somewhere from 4 to 8 percent royalties on every game sold. Depending on your contract, this may be based on the retail price of your game or on the wholesale price, which is a fraction of the retail price.

Freelance game design is also a job that comes with a lot of expenses that can outweigh your earnings, such as travel, conventions, making prototypes … it all adds up.

In order to get your games signed with publishers, you often have to make arrangements with them to meet, travel to conventions, and spend a fair chunk of money along the way.

Once you're more established and have some connections, it is much easier to reach out to publishers you know to see if they're interested in seeing your latest and greatest creations. But until that time, your success will depend at least somewhat on your ability and willingness to travel and meet with publishers face-to-face.

Sure, you can still reach out with a cold email and a sell sheet, and this does sometimes work, however, having that in-person connection and being able to put a face to a name is that much more powerful. But all this comes with a price, and you may quickly discover that you're spending more money to get those meetings with publishers than you'll earn in royalties from your game.

As I mentioned earlier in this chapter, you will likely have to supplement your income in some way. This may mean that you spend a lot less time actually designing games, yet if your intention is to one day work as a full-time game designer, this is a sacrifice you must be willing to make until you have a big enough name in the industry or have one of your games catch fire (hopefully not literally!).

Unless you can bank up savings that will last you through at least a couple of years or have a partner that can support you and your family financially while you are pursuing your dream, doing this on the side or having multiple other streams of income is critical.

Let's move on to some other roles in the industry that are lesser known, but just as important, and much more in demand.

2

Game Development

Another role that is crucial in the board game industry but is often overlooked and underappreciated is that of the game developer.

"But isn't that just the same thing as a game designer?" you might be asking. "Aren't the two terms interchangeable?"

While people often confuse them, there are some key distinctions between these two positions.

A game designer is responsible for all the creative aspects of the game. They were the ones to come up with the idea for the game. They thought up the theme, tested and tweaked the mechanics, playtested, and made improvements to the game play.

A game developer redesigns aspects of the game to make it into a more marketable product. They ask questions, like "Does this component need to be part of the game?", "Is this rule necessary?", and "Would removing this step make the game better?" They smooth out any rough edges and essentially take the game the last mile. This is often referred to as "dev work."

How I Landed "Dev" Work

One way to find "dev" work is to first become a good playtester. If you can get good at providing solid, actionable feedback in playtesting sessions, particularly when playtesting a game for a publisher, they will recognize how valuable you are.

This has happened to Peter C. Hayward, game designer and owner of Jellybean Games. He's landed development work from other publishers who appreciated the valuable feedback he provided at playtesting sessions.

DOI: 10.1201/9781003334408-4

In turn, Peter has seen my involvement in playtests and also knows that I've designed several fun, uncomplicated card games. When he was looking for someone to help him out with some development work for a hybrid card game, he had signed that used his Lady and the Tiger and Jabberwocky games together, I said I was interested. His response was, "Oh yeah, that would totally be your jam!"

So, he hired me to do the dev work on the game.

The first thing I did was print out the cards, gather some tokens, and learn the rules. Then I played the game a few times. It was a fun game; however, I immediately saw some potential issues, including too many rounds ending in a tie, too many restrictions on placing and moving tokens that caused them to often get stuck in one position, and a lack of escalation as the game progressed through the rounds.

Oh, the two games were already published as well, so I was limited to using only the existing components. I couldn't add a single new thing to the game.

So, I tried a few things. I introduced a betting system, a change to token placement mechanics, and an increase in tokens available each round. This led to more variation in scoring, more movement of the tokens (which made the timing of betting and the ability to bluff more exciting), and a nice escalation in gameplay over the three rounds.

I playtested this multiple times with different groups, making little tweaks to get the balance just right, then, I updated the rules and shared everything with Peter. I was in constant communication as I playtested, identifying issues I saw (which he had also identified), and letting him know the solutions I had come up with and was testing.

I've also volunteered to do free development work for others. This has even led to being asked to become a co-designer on multiple games. You never know what will come from helping out on a project!

Why Game Development Is So Valuable

A good game developer will be able to look at a game and determine what will make it a better game and a more marketable product. They may find ways to reduce or reuse components to bring the cost down. They need to be able to "trim the fat." A great game developer finds solutions for the many little problems in a game that may crop up from time to time.

For example, when I realized the production cost for *Relics of Rajavihara* was going to be higher than I wanted, I put on my developer hat. I was able to reduce the number of wooden blocks from 52 to 38, while also tightening up gameplay and reducing setup time. This saved me a lot of money on production costs, allowing me to reduce the price for potential backers without sacrificing quality.

Another example is the mega-hit, *Wingspan*. Jamey Stegmaier added the very thematic bird feeder dice tower to the game when he was developing the game. This added a really nice (and functional) component that gave *Wingspan* even more value.

Game developers will often find other issues, such as:

- Unclear rules
- Too many exceptions or "if-then" conditions
- Potentially unnecessary components
- Dominant strategies
- Unbalanced cards or player powers

Sometimes (actually, quite often) a game designer will be too close to their own game. They've playtested it a ton and may be reluctant to make more changes or just can't see an issue that exists. That's where a game developer comes in. They can look at a game more objectively and can see what a designer may not notice.

John Zinser, CEO and Director of Creative for AEG, says, "It seems that everyone entering the industry wants to be a game designer—and don't get me wrong we can always use more good designers. But I know many of our near peers are looking for excellent developers. Someone who can take a project that is at 80 percent and deliver it, press-ready, on a budget and on schedule."[1]

The demand is there. If you have the right skills and experience, there may be opportunities available for you.

So, now that we know what a game developer is and what they do, how does one go about getting a job as a game developer?

In-House Game Development

Some of the larger publishers will have a game developer—or even a team of game developers—on staff whose job is to take a game that's already been designed and make improvements to it.

However, there's only a handful of really big publishers that have full-time game developers. Most companies are much smaller than this and only have a few employees in total. They don't necessarily have the funds or the number of projects to warrant having a full-time game developer on the team.

That's where versatility comes in.

If you land a job with a publisher, you may get to do game development. But you might also be responsible for evaluating submissions, playtesting, demoing games, and working the convention booth, along with a slew of other tasks.

You'll see this as a common theme in this book and in the board game industry as a whole. You're often asked to take on several roles, so you need to be proficient in many skills.

The more you can do to help the publisher you're working for, the more you'll be appreciated, and the more you'll be recognized as an essential asset to the team (and in-demand in the industry).

However, as I mentioned, few big companies hire game developers, and in a smaller company, you'll likely have to do a lot more than just game development.

If you want to focus on game development full-time or even part-time, you can certainly connect with publishers to see if any positions are available, but just like with game design, you're more likely going to find more opportunities doing freelance work.

Freelance Game Development

If you work as a freelance game developer, you will be working with publishers on one-off projects, helping to make their games shine before they bring them to market. In order to make a decent wage, you'll need to network and become known to several different publishers.

You can either charge an hourly rate for your development time or work on a project-by-project basis. The latter option would involve you assessing a game and how much development work it needs, then quoting the publisher for the amount you feel is fair based on the amount of time and effort that would be necessary to fully develop the game. It will be up to the publisher to let you know their budget and for you to determine if you can work within their parameters.

But before you can get this gig, you have to prove to a publisher that you're capable of doing great development work. There are a few ways you can do this.

You could simply volunteer to help a publisher for free, letting them know you're building your portfolio and are willing to work for experience and to get some referrals. You probably want to have some kind of relationship with a publisher, at least have talked to them or volunteered with them, before you approach them with this kind of offer.

You can even reach out to creators in the community who are preparing to launch their game on Kickstarter. If you catch them at the right time, you may get their interest. I mean, how could they refuse some free development work?

Being active in the community, helping others, and offering your services are great ways to get noticed.

It may take a little time to build your reputation and your resume, but if you do this right, you'll land more and more gigs. Then you can start to reach out to publishers to offer your paid development services, mentioning your other projects, and sharing glowing recommendations along the way.

Also, publishers talk. If you become well known in the industry for being a strong game developer, word of mouth will get around and publishers will start coming to you! Make sure it's easy for them to find you by having a website and contact information they can access. It won't hurt to show off whom you've worked with in the past by putting some publisher logos and game names up there as well!

Branching Out

Sen-Foong Lim is a prolific game designer with over twenty-five published games under his belt. He also does a lot of development work. He has a great reputation for delivering results and being great to work with, so publishers often now reach out to ask him to do development work for them.

He also has credits as a writer for multiple Role-Playing Games (RPGs). However, he does all this on the side. He has a full-time job and two college- or university-bound children, so he doesn't expect to make the jump to full-time anytime soon. Sen ponders, "Perhaps when they're done and I retire to a country that has a lower cost of living. Retirement isn't too far away!"[2]

As with a lot of other roles in the industry which are not quite full-time, you may need to do other work or have multiple small jobs either within the industry (writer, editor, etc.) or outside of it to help pay the bills if there isn't enough dev work out there. Although it is a critical role, many creators who decide to self-publish—and even some publishers—don't give that much thought to game development. Many just try to do it themselves.

That means it's sometimes up to you to show them how important game development is by offering to lend a hand, building up your credentials, experience, and portfolio, then offering your game development services to others, showing them how much better you can make their game (you'll be even more valuable if you can help to find them ways to save money at the same time!).

In the next section, we're going to look at publishers, both what it's like to become one and what it's like to work for one (as a full-time employee or freelancer).

Section II

Publishing

3

Becoming a Board Game Publisher

There are hundreds of board game publishers out there. Some have been around for decades, whereas others are just figuring out how to launch their first game on Kickstarter.

A publisher, not to be confused with a manufacturer (which we'll talk about in Chapter 12), is responsible for getting a game made and out to customers in whatever way they see fit. They may sell their games via crowdfunding, retail, conventions, or more likely, some combination of these methods. They work with artists and graphic designers, along with other creators, to bring game projects to life. These could be games they have designed themselves (self-publishing), games they have licensed from other game designers, or some combination of the two.

Some publishers will be bought out. Others won't be here a year from now. It's a small, niche market compared to a lot of other industries, and while the competition is generally very friendly and helpful, it is still quite competitive.

I spoke with many different publishers to get their insights into the industry. We talked about many topics, including the existing roles in their company and the skills needed for them, their biggest surprises when they started out, and their advice for someone thinking about making the jump to a full-time career in the board game industry. All of the information and quotes contained here are from these interviews unless otherwise stated.

This chapter will go in-depth into what it takes to become a publisher. The chapter that follows will detail what it looks like to work for a publisher, which will be followed by individual chapters dedicated to different roles you might find within a game publishing company, beyond design and development.

DOI: 10.1201/9781003334408-6

So You Want to Be a Game Publisher?

In many ways, becoming a game publisher is much like starting any business. If you're working by yourself (which you often will be, at least at the start), you'll have to wear many hats.

You'll be handling customer service, logistics, working with freelancers and vendors, marketing, and all the other hundreds of things that go into running your own business.

Entrepreneurship isn't for everyone. It's a lot of hard work and you need to put in a lot of hours. You'll often lose money in the first year or two before you turn a profit (or close up shop).

In most cases, you'll be starting this as a side business. Just as with game design, very few people have the time and money to be able to go into game publishing as a full-time gig. Publishers often have a full-time job and put in a lot of time on weekends, evenings, and any other time they can find to get things up and running.

And there's a lot more involved than meets the eye. As Jason Schneider, VP of Product Development at Gamewright, puts it, he didn't expect he'd "have to continually make one thousand tiny decisions about every aspect of a product during its creation."[3]

It isn't easy. But if you're willing to put in a lot of work, make lots of mistakes along the way, and learn from these mistakes so you can grow and become a better business owner, it can be very rewarding.

Just don't expect to strike it rich overnight. Or at all.

Most of the publishers I spoke with talked about leaving much higher-paying jobs to either start their game company or work high up within one. They took a pay cut to do what they love. So, if you're in it for the money, you've probably chosen the wrong profession! However, with a lot of hard work and a keen eye for amazing games that will sell well on the market, you *can* make a living as a publisher.

If your passion for games outweighs everything else and you're willing and able to get by on a lesser salary than you might earn elsewhere, working in the game industry, whether as a publisher or in another role, can be very fulfilling.

Everyone working in the game industry is in it for the love of the game. They love playing games and sharing this experience with others. They've met some amazing people within the industry and many of their closest relationships are with those associated with the hobby.

Being able to travel, meet amazing people (fans and others working in the industry), and play lots of incredible new games are among the unexpected and very welcome benefits of working in this industry.

In other words, you might not get rich monetarily, but there is a good chance you could end up rich in friendship and happiness. A good way to achieve this kind of wealth is through game publishing—so let's see if this profession is right for you.

The Skills Needed to Make It as a Game Publisher

Those who get into game publishing, whether as the sole proprietor of their own company or working in a key position within an established company, come from diverse backgrounds.

Many come from completely different industries, from retail to graphic design to advertising to children's television production. A few worked in product development before moving into board games, which translates well into game development and publishing. Others moved over from video games, marketing companies, or were serial entrepreneurs. Despite the diversity, one thing remained universally true: the specific industry or position someone came from before getting into board game publishing mattered much less than the skills and experience they brought to the table.

Running a business on your own requires a diverse skill set. When you're doing everything by yourself, you have to be good at a lot of different things or take the time to develop these skills. You may be able to farm some jobs out; however, when you're just getting started, you may not have the money to do this, so you'll often have to figure out most everything on your own.

This takes a lot of effort, so you have to have a **strong work ethic**. You have to be curious, always wanting to learn more, and willing to try different things. It takes a lot of drive and a willingness to push through, even when things aren't going well, to succeed.

You need to have **good business sense**. You must be able to design or pick great games that fit your brand and audience that you will be able to sell. You must also be willing to take some calculated risks—risky enough that the payoff is worth taking the chance, but not so risky that failure will lead to the collapse of your business.

You must be able to not only identify a great game but also to find the right artists to make that game stand out and look amazing. Then you must partner with trustworthy manufacturers, fulfillment companies, and distributors that will get your games into the hands of all your fans.

You must be a **great communicator**. You need to work with game designers, developers, artists, graphic designers, distributors, stores, convention organizers, and customers to be successful, so, you need to be a good listener, as well as be able to convey what you need from others in a very clear and respectful manner.

Problem-solving is another key skill. You'll have to make a ton of decisions about your games, your company, and everything that goes into running your own business day to day. Problems will often arise, and you'll have to be able to identify the root cause and best course of action. Sometimes your first solution won't work, but you can't just give up. You have to keep trying until you get it right.

Time management is also critical. You need to be able to plan a project and deliver on time, taking care of all the details that go into a successful launch. You need to keep on top of all the business decisions that must be made and not waste time on the things that don't matter as much.

Marketing and promotion don't come naturally to a lot of people, but they have to become second nature to you if you're going to be successful. As Adam McCrimmon, CEO of XYZ Game Labs notes, "As a publisher, I spend way more time on promotion, marketing and product design compared to game design and other more glamorous tasks." This was his biggest surprise after he and his partners started their company.

Running a Kickstarter campaign, managing a booth at a big convention, or releasing a new game into the wild are not enough. People need to know your game is out there or is about to be released, and they have to be genuinely excited about it. For that to happen, you need to be able and willing to get the word out and build up that excitement, whatever it takes.

As Justin De Witt, co-founder of Fireside Games, notes, "The biggest surprise was probably how much the day-to-day minutia of running a business can be overwhelming. I think this is something people overlook when getting into publishing. You are starting a very complicated small business and that means dealing with issues like customer service, bookkeeping, accounting, copyrights, international shipping and safety testing, contracts, maybe getting loans, etc. These take up far more of your time than you'd expect... It's not just making games all day long."[4]

Sure, you might be good at picking a great game and developing it further, but if you can't communicate well with others, network and get your games into distribution, and figure out how to market your game as a product, it will be very difficult to stay in business.

How to Get Started as a Publisher

If all of this excites you rather than scares you off, and you still want to open up your own board game publishing company, then let's talk about how to make this happen! I will just touch on this briefly here, as a whole book would be needed to explain how to run a successful board game publishing company.

As with any other business, you'll want to come up with a name and register your company. The process may vary depending on your country and state/province, so you'll need to do a little research to determine what steps are needed to open a business in your region.

If you're in the US, many recommend registering your company as a Limited Liability Corporation (LLC). In other countries, it may be a matter of registering as a corporation. This will keep your personal and business matters separate. Look into what your options are where you live.

The registration process will inevitably involve filling out a bunch of forms and will likely include paying a small registration fee. Once this is all done and you've received confirmation that your company has been registered, you're pretty much ready to go!

Now, it's up to you to either continue to develop and market your own game in preparation for Kickstarter or another sales method if you're self-publishing (which is how most publishers start out) or start hunting for new games to sign.

Transitioning from Designer to Publisher

If you're getting into publishing, chances are it's because you've already designed a game and have chosen to self-publish. This will give you some experience and allows you to develop your skills as a publisher, learning the ropes when it comes to marketing, logistics, and everything else involved in taking a game to market.

Once you have some small successes under your belt, you can continue to design and publish your own games (which is a lot of work, trying to do everything involved in the process) or start signing games from other designers, letting them focus on the game itself while you put your attention into finding an audience for that game and making it a success.

You'll likely be starting out with little or no money, so you'll have to find creative ways to stretch those dollars and demo your games to as many people as you can without breaking the bank. Anywhere you advertise or spend money will have to provide a good return on investment (ROI). You might rent a booth at a convention, spend money on Facebook ads, or try a more organic approach, playing your game wherever your audience hangs out or connecting with others in online groups. Finding ways to build an audience often involves a lot of trial and error.

After your first game or two, you'll see how much work this is. Some will decide not to continue, whereas others will be excited about the possibilities that lie ahead. They will press on, continue to work hard and build their audience one fan at a time.

I won't lie, and neither will the other publishers I spoke with: It is a *lot* of hard work, long days, and slow growth before you start to see a lot of progress.

Curt Covert, the founder of Smirk & Dagger Games, confesses, "I knew it was going to be hard to make a living publishing board games. I never knew how hard. It is the unexpected, unforeseeable challenges that people never consider. Many are outside of one's control. Printing/product issues. Logistical nightmares. Shipping headaches. And the sudden and drastic shortening of a game's shelf life in recent years. You have all the same challenges as any other small business, but with a very time-intensive development cycle, serving a relatively niche audience (as compared to other US small businesses)."[5]

It's challenging, and the market is always changing. With the advent of Kickstarter, more games are now available to gamers than ever before (by a huge factor). This "cult of the new" is very much a reality, and it means that games no longer keep people's interests like they used to. New titles often only stay in people's minds for weeks, not months or years.

You have to be ready to adapt, change course, and figure out how to get your small slice of a pie that's constantly being divided into more and more pieces.

Adam McCrimmon, the CEO of XYZ Game Labs, is part of a small four-person team. He is primarily a publisher, but his role also includes design and marketing. Even still, he's not doing this full time...yet. He has a day job as a digital strategist. He realizes that you can't necessarily jump into the industry full time and expect to make a decent living right away. It takes time.

As Adam puts it, "Set your expectations first. As with most industries, you're going to have to spend some time there before you start to make any traction."[6]

Not all will succeed, and most would certainly be able to earn a better living in another industry—but those who make it will find a lot of fulfillment in this amazing hobby!

4

Working for a Board Game Publisher

Many publishers are small and have very few employees. Some of the larger ones (think Hasbro and Spin Master) may have large teams dedicated to designing, developing, marketing, and all the other aspects of producing games.

Smaller publishers rely quite a bit on freelancers (game designers, artists, graphic designers, story writers, rulebook editors, etc.), as they do not have the money to hire people full time, nor the amount of ongoing work needed to employ many people in different positions.

The few employees they do have need to be good at a multitude of tasks. Even though you might be the Director of Sales and Marketing, you might also be called upon to playtest and develop games, work at the convention booth, run the company's social media accounts, and do a whole bunch of other things you wouldn't normally associate with your title.

That means, while one or two skills get you in the door, it will be the ability and willingness to learn, adapt, and help out wherever you can—as well as get proficient at multiple things—that will keep you in that job. If you can help a publisher to develop and release great games that people love, the company will have much more success and growth, and your job will be that much more secure.

But then again, if you're looking for stability and security, this may not be the industry for you. Profit margins are razor-thin, and the ability for a company to stay afloat relies on each game they release doing well (or at least one being a big enough hit to balance the others).

People come and go. There was a stretch of about two weeks last year where I was following up with three publishers about prototypes I had given to them months before. I found out that all three of the people I had been in

DOI: 10.1201/9781003334408-7

contact with and had taken my prototype were no longer with the company. I don't know if it was the decision of the employee or the employer, but in any case, there is a fair bit of turnaround within the industry, for sure.

Many publishing companies are started from the ground up by a small group of colleagues or friends from either inside or outside of the industry. Until they grow and expand to the point where they are seeing gaps in their own company and have the funds to hire someone new, it might be difficult to get a job in their organization.

Let's take a look at how to get in with one of these publishers. Many publishers I connected with suggested that most jobs get filled by people with the skills that are in demand, and who can show a company how they will help them grow. Most of these people are known to the publisher before there is any discussion of hiring.

Publishers pay attention to people who show promise and are eager to help. If you volunteer to work at a publisher's booth, playtest a game, review and edit a rule book, or offer another valuable service (especially for free—at least at the start) and do a great job, they will remember you.

Again, a lot of the jobs will be freelance, but enough freelance work can translate into the ability to make a living.

But we'll get to freelancing a little later in the book. For now, let's look at jobs that exist within publishing companies and what skills are needed in these important roles.

5

Product Development & Project Management

Product development or project management will often be handled by the owner (or one of the owners) of the company, at least until the company has grown and is hiring other employees. When this role is hired out, it comes with great responsibility and oversight. It's really up to you to ensure every product you put out is reflective of the company, is high quality, and will delight their fans.

You'll be responsible for ensuring that the games you choose to sign are a good match, the look and style of the game as a product is just right, and your message is consistent and clear.

The role of a product developer or project manager is more common than many other positions in the industry. There is a need, even in small companies, to turn those games into products that will sell.

Scott Gaeta is the owner of Renegade Games, the company behind hit games like *Clank!* And *Raiders of the North Sea*. He considers his role to be that of a Producer or Brand Manager. It's his responsibility to ensure that everything is running smoothly and that decisions are made based on the brand that he has created for Renegade Games, which is focused on family-friendly strategy games.

When I told him about my idea to write this book and how he inspired me to do so, Scott was enthusiastic. He said "It's a very overlooked topic and the industry needs good people in all roles."[7]

As I've mentioned, when you're working for a publisher, you often have to wear many hats. You'll be responsible for more than one thing, but your overall goal will always be to help the company succeed in its vision in whatever way you can best help.

DOI: 10.1201/9781003334408-8

There are three traits Scott specifically mentioned that are the most important for those looking for a career in the board game industry:

- Experience
- Work Ethic
- Networking[8]

A lot of jobs in the industry are not advertised. Companies are looking to fill roles with just the right people, based on their reputation and work ethic. Sometimes you have to show them just how invaluable you are and make them wonder how they ever got along without you!

Networking Leads to Becoming a Game Producer

Fertessa Allyse is a Game Producer at Funko Games, a role she recently acquired. Her main responsibilities are helping with game design and development, along with making sure that games are sticking to their timelines. Fertessa has worked on several family-friendly games for Funko, but isn't able to disclose her projects just yet.

But how did she find out about and land such an important role?

In Fertessa's words, "I was very active in conventions, online conventions, and online playtesting communities, and would always play other peoples' games (both online and in-person) and try to give thoughtful feedback. This made it easier for me to get playtesters in return. If I was asked to speak on a panel or do an event, and I was able, then I did it."[9]

Funko makes games for the mass market, so it's not the kind of role that most publishers have. However, there are opportunities if you know where to look. Fertessa got noticed because she was putting herself out there, being active in the community, and helping others. Take note of this!

She goes on to say, "I would never have gotten as far as I did without so many people supporting me and reaching out to me. A lot of these opportunities came to me because people I'd connected with on Twitter heard about a thing and pinged me to make sure I'd heard about it too. More than half of the opportunities I took were because people approached me and made me aware of them. I just followed through, and thankfully, that usually led to more opportunities."[9]

Since she was always so helpful to others and was able to showcase her talents naturally, others wanted to support her efforts.

The one thing Fertessa is quick to mention is that these opportunities do come with some drawbacks. For example, due to her contract with Funko, she is now unable to work on independent games. All her designs have to be for the publisher she works for.[9]

This is something to keep in mind, as some publishers, particularly the larger ones, may not allow you to work independently on your own games. Smaller publishers may be more flexible. They may want the right of first refusal, and if they pass, you are free to do what you like with your game. Others may be completely open to other endeavors. That's a conversation you'll have to have with the publisher if you're thinking of joining their team.

From Accountant to Project Manager for a Major Board Game Publisher

Jean-Baptiste Ramassamy is a project manager for Ravensburger. I met him through pitching a number of my games to his company during an event called Ravensburger Inventor Days, which was a series of days dedicated to designers pitching games to Ravensburger. I asked him about how he landed this role along with his responsibilities.

Before joining Ravensburger, Jean-Baptiste held roles in other companies as an accountant and financial auditor. His passion for board games, along with project-management skills from previous roles, helped him land the job.[10]

He lists his responsibilities as follows:

1. "Meet inventors and select games
2. Playtesting to improve game mechanics
3. Turn these ideas into products (project development)
4. Write rules
5. Commercial sheets, samples, and catalog texts/images
6. Introduce games to buyers
7. Communication strategy and tools
8. Build relationships with bloggers"[10]

Jean-Baptiste admits, "There is far more administration, box/contents sampling and small uninteresting tasks than I expected. The border between passion and work is also sometimes difficult to see."[10] But his passion for games and ability to connect with others he admires in the industry are what keep him going.

His closing thoughts were, "It's not about playing and making cool stuff all the time, it's a real job. Sometimes you will hate it, sometimes you will adore it!"[10]

A Joshua of All Trades

I met Joshua Lobkowicz at PAX Unplugged in 2019 when I was pitching a few of my games to Grey Fox Games. Joshua is the Head of Game Development and Acquisition there, as well as the CEO of his own small publishing company, Travel Buddy Games.

Joshua started at Grey Fox Games as an editor for their rulebooks and components, then advanced to the role of game developer before being promoted to his current position. He studied literature and language in college and feels that the critical thinking and analytical skills he developed there have helped him in game development.[11]

Joshua says, "In game development I find that being something of a jack of all trades is incredibly useful. I work with designers to bring the games forward and it helps for me to be able to back off on the things they are great at and focus on the things they are not."[11]

He is good at both bringing out the theme of a game where the designer was more focused on the mechanics, as well as balancing a game with much-needed rules where the designer focused more on the theme, art, or story.

Writing and sending rejection letters is one of the toughest parts of his job. They receive hundreds of game submissions but only publish four to six each year, and it's never easy having to tell a designer that their game doesn't fit with Grey Fox's catalog.

Joshua also shared his advice for anyone looking to break into the industry: "Work convention booths. It will not only allow you to make connections with people in the industry but it will let you begin to peek behind the curtain and see what the industry is like from the inside."[11]

Sometimes It's Who You Know

Sydney Engelstein is the Director of Game Development for Indie Game Studios. I met her a couple of years ago at Origins Game Fair, when I was pitching my game, *Mayan Curse*, to her company.

Sydney identified networking and previous game design experience as the biggest reasons she landed her role. She had multiple games published with Stronghold Games and a good relationship with the owner, Stephen Buonocore. So, when she heard that Stronghold would be merging with Indie Boards and Cards, she asked if that meant new positions would be created. It turned out she was right, and after applying for the position, being interviewed, meeting with the team, and doing some development and rulebook writing for a prototype they would be publishing, she landed the job.

Being a small company, she has had to wear many hats; among other things, Sydney does development work, project management, and writing—something she didn't anticipate when she first joined. Writing is something she enjoys, and since nobody else was really that interested, she has taken on the writing for rulebooks and marketing, which she takes delight in. She appreciates getting paid to do what she loves to do!

Sydney is also able to work on some games and expansions from the ground up. If there is an existing game in their catalog and the owners want to develop something new in that world, she often has the opportunity to work on that project.

There's also a lot of editing, organizing, and "busy work." She admits the pay isn't great, but she loves the writing aspect of her job and working with her team, and she can also work on her own games independently—Indie Game Studios just has the right of first refusal. However, like a professional chef coming home and having to cook dinner, she rarely feels like working on a game of her own after working on other people's games all day long![12]

Sydney's success in landing her role goes to show that networking and experience designing games can definitely help get your foot in the door.

She strongly recommends building good relationships. "My advice would really be to network. Get a few things under your belt in your chosen field like a few published board games or a podcast for marketing or whatever will show your skills and then go to conventions and make friends and be kind and passionate and keep in touch with publishers you work with. People are far more likely to turn to a name they recognize than one they don't."[12]

The Chief Wizard Joins the Board Game Industry

Debbie Moynihan is the Chief Operating Officer (COO) for White Wizard Games. She started out as a marketing consultant for the company, which is run by her husband, Rob Dougherty.

She was in management and high-level positions for multiple start-ups and big-name tech companies before transitioning to full-time with White Wizard Games. Debbie brings her hands-on experience and skills in marketing, project management, team building, and other management skills to the industry.

Now, she is responsible for most of the operations outside of game design and development at White Wizard Games.

When asked what skills were the most vital in her role, Debbie said "Management and marketing skills, problem-solving skills, communication skills, ability to learn new things quickly, ability to multitask, and strong work ethic."[13]

Debbie makes a good living in her role but admits she only earns a fraction of what she used to make in her previous role as VP of Marketing for some high-growth start-ups. However, she values passion and flexibility over money and was able to make the transition because she was in a good financial position to do so.

She recommends having another career outside the industry to make ends meet as a starting point before making the leap to full time in the industry and that you "Get as much practical experience as you can and meet as many people as you can."[13]

From Television Production to Game Production

Jason Schneider is the VP of Product Development for Gamewright, the company behind the hit games *Sushi Go* and *Forbidden Island*, among others.

I've been in touch with Jason ever since I pitched a game to his company several years ago. He even contributed to my second book, *The Board Game Designer's Guide to Getting Published*, providing some great advice and insights on what his company is looking for.

He worked his way up to his current VP position after working as their Sales & Marketing Coordinator, followed by a stint as Director of Product Development and Marketing. He previously worked in children's television production.

Jason believes that getting into his role or any other role in the industry has little to do with your educational background and is more about having the right skills and experience. He says "I don't really look at education when considering people for new positions. I'm more interested in who they are as a person and what they bring to the table in terms of spirit and energy."[3]

He highlights the following as key contributors to his success thus far:

1. "Being curious
2. Being a good listener
3. Being a good problem solver
4. Being able to see the forest through the trees"[3]

Jason is responsible for all the little things that go into making a game and turning it into a marketable product.

Are you beginning to see a common theme here?

Pretty much everyone we've heard from who is involved in product development and project management is responsible for turning a great game into a great product. That's a huge part of publishing that designers don't always consider, but should.

When I asked Jason if he would recommend a career change into board games, he said, "…if you're passionate about board games and really think that this is your calling—go for it. On the other hand, understand that all is not aces behind the 'cardboard curtain.' Sometimes it's better not knowing how the sauce gets made."[3]

Finding an Opportunity

I also reached out to Patrick Marino, who is the Game Design Manager at The Op. Before working for the publisher, Patrick designed games in his free time and pitched them to publishers, including some that he pitched to The Op. He developed a relationship with the publisher through both pitching and hosting local playtesting events.

In 2017, he was approached by The Op about working on a hobby game project and the discussion turned into a conversation about a full-time position. Patrick was soon interviewed and hired as their new Game Design Manager.

In his role, Patrick works with the content development team to come up with new product ideas and then helps to design and develop them. He also evaluates outside submissions.

When it comes to landing a role in the industry, Patrick says "There are two major entry points I suggest. The first is freelance work to build design skills and begin to demonstrate to publishers that you are professional and can produce consistent quality work. The second is getting involved as a volunteer. One way to volunteer is as a playtester for a publisher, The Op has a great online community of testers, and you can sign-up on our website TheOp.games. The other way to volunteer is to offer booth support during major conventions. Some publishers will cover expenses for volunteers who help teach games at the shows. The Envoy program from Double Exposure is a great place to start."[14]

Patrick was fortunate to land a full-time position, which allowed him to leave his job in higher education. He admits there are few publishers offering jobs, so the competition can be tough. He also works on all his own game ideas internally but feels he gets to work on many more games that will actually make it out the door as finished products than he would as a freelancer.[14]

I wanted to note that it's really up to the company what title they use for all these roles and others that we'll get into in the upcoming chapters. Some publishers may create manager positions and others will call them directors. Slightly larger publishers may have VP roles or even "C-level" positions (like COO). Director is a very important-sounding role and is above that of a manager, so small companies will often have a lot of directors, but no managers under them. Being a director in a small company is often more similar to a management role in a larger firm.

If you're passionate about board games and have a lot of skills and/or experience related to bringing products to market successfully, a role in project management or product development may be a great fit for you.

Now, let's look at some other more specialized positions.

6

Communications/Marketing/Sales

A publisher's success in being able to get the word out about their newest release depends a lot on marketing and communications. Nowadays, a publisher must have some form of social media presence to get people excited about their latest and greatest game.

They also have to develop and deliver on plans for getting their games out to fans, whether through Kickstarter, retail distribution, online sales, conventions, or, as is often the case, a combination of many of these approaches.

So, it's no surprise that many publishers indicated sales and marketing as the biggest gap in the industry and the role that is most needed.

If you have the right skills, you could find yourself in high demand. If you have experience in communications, sales, and/or marketing in another industry, you might be able to land a job with a board game publisher doing a similar role. However, don't expect the pay to be as high as it would be in a Fortune 500 company!

However, many publishing companies are small operations and employees have to wear many hats, sometimes doing multiple tasks like customer service, social media coordination, marketing, and sales. All these responsibilities may fall on one or more members of the team.

Stonemaier Games Hires Their Second Employee

One role that is becoming more and more relevant today involves promotion, particularly through email and social media channels. In fact, Jamey Stegmaier, owner of Stonemaier Games, after many years of being the only full-time employee finally made his first hire—Joe Aubrey. His role was the Director of Communications.

DOI: 10.1201/9781003334408-9

So, how did Joe land this job with such a respected publisher and industry expert?

Joe says, "I knew Jamey and volunteered my time at Stonemaier events, as well as played an active role teaching games at his weekly game nights (before the COVID-19 pandemic). This followed with a formal interview process and at least one other person being considered for the job."[15]

But while much of his role involves a lot of customer service and audience engagement, working for a publisher with only two full-time employees at the time of his hire (they are now up to three) means his tasks are always different from one day to the next. He's responsible for getting things done that Jamey doesn't have the time for or would prefer to delegate, but he also has a lot of autonomy in his job and is free to make the choices he believes are in the best interest of the company.

Joe believes that his skills are very transferable within the industry, but feels that he has a lot more control and variety in his day working for Stonemaier Games than he would if he were to transition to another company.[15]

Stonemaier Grows Again

Jamey's second hire was Alexander Schmidt. He had previously been employed at Greater Than Games and was already working closely with Stonemaier Games for their logistics and sales.

After high school, Alexander decided that he wanted to work in the board game industry. He'd been a tabletop gamer his whole life. He said that he had creative, problem-solving, and project-management skills, but no education related to these. He didn't know how he would use these skills to land a job.

So, he started networking.

He attended local conventions and events, where he quickly got to know both Stonemaier Games and Greater Than Games and struck up friendships with both. When trouble struck Greater Than Games and they were having difficulties getting Stonemaier's game, *Charterstone,* out into distribution, they called Alexander for help. This evolved into a full-time position as Account Manager, liaising between the two companies.

Alexander was a natural fit for Stonemaier Games when Jamey decided that it was time to hire his third employee for the position of Director of Sales.

Alexander says "Especially for a small company, hiring someone is incredibly risky. The better they know you, the more they know what they're getting from you, which decreases the risk."[16]

So, the better you can get to know about a publisher or any other company in the industry and show them what you're capable of, the higher the odds will be that they will consider you for that new role they need to fill. Stepping up within a company to learn a new skill or take over a task that someone else needs to delegate is also a great way to become more knowledgeable and in demand, while also showing your employer that you take initiative and want to help the company grow and prosper.

Alexander says he is responsible for "Keeping up communication with our distribution, retail, and localization partners, to make sure I'm communicating deadlines and managing orders and estimates from them. Keeping track of all of our product in warehouses and production and making informed decisions about sales and printing."[16]

He says that written and oral communication, along with a good understanding of logistics, data management, and spreadsheets are the skills that have helped him most in this role. You'll see a little later in the book how these same skills apply on the other side in logistics and fulfillment companies, like where Alexander got his start.

Alexander is also quick to mention that it's a lot of hard work. It's not just playing board games all day. You've been hired to do a job and you have to do what you've been hired to do. You may get opportunities to playtest, do some development work, etc., but there are no guarantees.

Alexander reminds us, "Ultimately the job you're taking is the job you're doing, not 'board games'. You need to be happy with that job."[16]

Marketing Wizard

Rachael Blaske is the VP of Channel Marketing for White Wizard Games. Her job involves building and maintaining relationships with distributors, retailers, and foreign partners. She also creates marketing content and helps develop timelines for product releases. She says she's "All about communication."[17]

Prior to joining White Wizard Games, Rachael was the CEO of Five24 Labs. She started out in customer service and worked her way up to eventually run the company.

Rachael's role at White Wizard Games involves a lot of sales and marketing, which she says her talents really lie in. Networking and talking with others come naturally to Rachael and she'd made a lot of connections in this way. She also feels her skills are very transferable should she think of working for another company in the future.

When I asked her what entry-level jobs or roles she would suggest for someone trying to break into the industry, she recommended "Demo staff. It is a great way to get to know publishers and that goes both ways."[17]

Helping publishers out at a convention by demoing their games and getting new customers excited about a game is a great way to help a publisher and make some new connections.

A Serial Entrepreneur Enters the World of Board Games

Finally, John Zinser, CEO and Director of Creative for AEG, says that he owned and ran a number of different businesses before starting a board game publishing company.

However, the experience he got from running a golf-marketing company was the biggest benefit to him leading into this new venture. John says, "My golf-marketing business was a whole bunch of cold calling and learning how to sell. It helped me when we started selling games and selling advertising in Shadis magazine."[1]

Again, understanding sales is such an important and under-recognized role. You can have the greatest game in the world, but if you can't convince stores to sell it and customers to try it or buy it, you won't have much of a business.

John goes on to say "Most salespeople in our industry are not selling, they are managing the flow of information. Having someone on the phone cold calling stores and just saying hi and getting information about their games works, but it is hard work. Most people give up after one or two weeks."[1]

While most publishers have few staff and hiring opportunities, if you can prove to a publisher that you can help them to generate a lot more sales, and that hiring you will practically pay for itself, why wouldn't they consider you?

John's advice for getting into the industry is as follows: "I would suggest that you not be afraid to start at the bottom. Getting into the gates is the first most important step. Once you have any job, volunteer or paid, you likely will have access to the inner workings of the company. Then you can find ways to make yourself indispensable."[1]

If sales, social media, and marketing come naturally to you and you love board games, there are huge opportunities and needs to be filled within the board game industry.

However, if selling and marketing don't come naturally to you, you might want to consider one of the other many opportunities within publishing companies that we'll get into in the next chapter.

7

Other Roles Within a Publishing Company

While we've touched on many of the main roles you might see with different board game publishers, others are lesser-known and may only exist within a smaller number of companies.

Acquisitions (or "Scout")

A person in this role would be responsible for reviewing submissions, meeting with designers, requesting prototypes, and bringing them back to the publisher for evaluation. They may also be involved in testing and evaluating a game for the publisher.

A role such as this is often on contract and maybe only considered a part-time position. In other companies, there will be one or more people who have this as just one part of their job description. Often, a game developer will also be tasked with reviewing and evaluating game submissions, as they will be the ones to further develop a game if the publisher decides to sign it.

Darren Watts, who consults for Chronicle Books (they have a game division), attends conventions and other events, meets with designers, and evaluates whether their games would be a good fit for Chronicle. Any games that would make a good match are then sent on to the publisher to evaluate further.

It's not a common role on its own, but may be found in larger publishers. If you're the type of person who likes to travel and meet others, have a good eye for potential products, and aren't afraid to tell people "no," this is a good role to consider.

Art Director/Creative Director

Anne-Marie De Witt is the CEO and co-owner of Fireside Games, along with her husband Justin. They are probably best known for their hit co-op game, *Castle Panic*. She handles all the business functions, as well as sales and marketing for Fireside Games. I've pitched a few games to them over the years, and although we've not found the perfect match yet, they have always been great to talk to and learn from.

Anne-Marie suggests that the positions of Art Director and Print Buyer are badly needed within the industry. When I asked her what skills are most needed in these roles, she replied "Art Director: an eye and language for establishing the visual style of a game and the ability to direct and manage freelance artists; Print Buyer: ability to suggest and request a variety of print materials, knowledge of manufacturing processes, and analysis of bids."[18]

Fortunately for them, Justin, whose title is Chief Creative Officer, fills the Art Director role nicely. He has a strong background in graphic design and multimedia, so he handles all the graphic design and layout for their games, directs other artists they work with, and is involved in all stages in the production of their games.

Once again, in a small company, one person may have to act not only as Art Director but also a variety of other roles as well. Only the larger, more well-established publishers will have roles dedicated solely to art direction.

Justin says "My degree in Graphic Design and Illustration was key in getting me into art related jobs early in my career. The creativity, problem-solving, and teamwork skills I picked up there helped prepare me for a lot of the production work I would need for the game industry. Additionally, the design/refine/repeat cycle of work that is often needed in solving Graphic Design problems is parallel to the workflow in designing a board game. That was a skill that was easy to transfer over."[4]

Justin also shared his very realistic thoughts on trying to land a job in the industry: "I also think it's important to understand that this industry is still incredibly niche. There are a handful of large, well-known companies that have impressive annual revenues, and do offer traditional jobs. After that it quickly drops down to very small companies that run extremely thin margins, often run by just two to five people, that don't have the means to employ any more staff. Set your expectations realistically."[4]

Still, the role of Art Director may be right for you if you have a degree and experience with visual arts and graphic design.

Finances

If you're good with money and numbers, you might want to look at roles in the industry related to finance.

It's unlikely that any smaller publishers will have a role strictly related to finance, and anything related to this will likely be wrapped up along with other responsibilities into another role, but there may be opportunities within one of the larger companies.

Your responsibilities would likely revolve around bookkeeping, tracking product sales, and ensuring vendors and contractors are paid on time (as well as ensuring your own company is getting paid).

The More Likely Scenario

While there is a small chance that a larger publisher will have these or other roles available, the likelihood is that these roles would either be contracted out or be just one aspect of another role.

Many of the publishers and industry professionals I connected with suggested looking at what you enjoy and are good at doing and start doing this on the side as a freelancer.

Jamey Stegmaier, who runs Stonemaier Games, said that one of the biggest realities of his job that he hadn't anticipated is "most of it is project management."[19] It's not all making games and having fun. A lot of work goes into running a company or working for one in the board game industry.

Jamey's advice for anyone trying to get into the industry is to find a problem that a company is facing and show them how you can help them to make improvements using your skills and experience. This is a great way to get your foot in the door, whether it is trying to land a job or a freelance gig.[19]

Vincent Vergonjeanne, who runs Lucky Duck Games, says, "Get good at one thing, expert-good, and you will become irreplaceable to whichever team hires you."[20]

While many people in the industry caution against trying to find work in the industry full time—and with good reason, based on the market changes, ambiguity, instability, and small margins—others, like Vincent, say, "If you have the opportunity, do it! There is nothing more rewarding than working in a field that provides so much joy to people."[20]

So, if you're still reading this book and you're still interested in working in the industry but maybe can't find a role with a publisher or prefer the freedom and flexibility of working with whom you want, when you want, keep reading!

The next section will look at the many different freelance roles in the industry that require specific skill sets that might be a great match for you.

Section III

Freelancing

8

True Stories of How Being Helpful Landed Paying Gigs

Gabe Barrett, who runs the Board Game Design Lab and also contributed his thoughts to this book, has mentioned many times in his podcast how a graphic designer, Drew Corkill, did some designs for him for free when Drew was trying to break into the industry. Gabe liked them so much that, before you knew it, he had hired Drew to do the graphic design for multiple games, books, and his website.

I was impressed by Drew as well, and I hired him to do the cover and formatting of my last two books (and this one as well!).

Sometimes good things happen when we do something nice for another person with no expectations.

Now this is just one story, and it only landed occasional freelance work, but you can see how word of mouth helped Drew, and more work came his way.

A Quick Mock-Up Leads to Paid Work

Something similar also happened to me recently. I had reached out to a number of game designers on my email list whom I felt would be interested in a course I was planning on re-launching. I wanted to see if the offer was interesting and if there was anything else they'd like to see as part of the course.

One aspiring game designer, Mitch Morris, reached out to me with some advice I wasn't expecting. He is a graphic designer by trade, so he was looking at this from a different perspective. He had some suggestions on how I could

DOI: 10.1201/9781003334408-12

shorten the page to give it more punch, as well as improve the layout of the page and separate the sections more effectively.

He even went so far as to make a quick mock-up of what the start of the page might look like with a different color scheme, and also put together a couple logos that I could use on the page. He offered to let me use them for free! I couldn't believe all the work he had done.

I could tell Mitch knew what he was doing, and I asked him if he'd like to redesign the page for me and what he would charge for the job. He came back with a reasonable offer and we started working on it together right away. He ended the email by saying he was surprised I made the offer, but was glad to help and got to work on the page immediately.

Mitch did an amazing job on my page, and I expect to hire him for more work in the future. He showed me that he could do something that would benefit me and would likely bring in even more interested game designers to my course. That was a great return on investment for me.

If you can do something for a publisher that makes them say, "Wow! That's something that will take our company to the next level," then you've got their attention. Plus, they will recommend you to other companies.

From Backer to Contributor

When I was running the Kickstarter campaign for *Relics of Rajavihara*, I was amazed by the generosity of my backers.

One of my stretch goals was custom meeples (people shaped pawns used in many games, first coined in 2000 to refer to the pawns used in Carcassonne). I posted a picture of what they might look like based on an image from another game. One of my backers, Cristo Daniel, had another idea. He took it upon himself to design two really cool meeple designs and offered to let me use them for free. I had never expected this! He didn't even want anything in return. One looked like an adventurer, similar to Indiana Jones (perfect from my protagonist), and the other was a caped villain, which suited the nemesis. I was glad to be able to use Cristo's upgrades to make the game even more appealing.

Later on, when I was doing some work on the expansion for the game, I knew exactly who to ask when I needed a couple more custom meeples. He created some amazing new designs and refused to take any money for them. At the very least, I'm making sure he gets a free copy of the expansion!

Cristo is building a great reputation and I'm sure he could turn this into part-time freelance work if he chose to. I know I will recommend him to others any chance I get.

Jeff Rules

I also recommend Jeff Fraser, who did an amazing job on the *Relics of Rajavihara* rulebook, all the time. Most of his business is word-of-mouth. He doesn't like to toot his own horn and he doesn't even need to (although he should, since he does a great job!). Now he's being recommended to so many game designers and publishers, he sometimes has to turn away work.

And it all started by working on rulebooks for a few publishers and showing them how much clearer he can communicate how to play a game than the designer or publisher can. This makes it easier for players to play the game and share the experience with others. A bad rulebook can lead to players giving up and posting negative reviews, but a good rulebook just makes the experience so much more welcoming.

What skills do you have that would benefit a publisher? What is something you can do better than a lot of other people?

If you can identify a skill of yours that publishers would find invaluable, you might just have a path into the board game industry.

9

Graphic Designer

I've tried to be very transparent about the fact that many of the jobs available in the board game industry are more likely to be freelance rather than full-time. It's just the nature of the industry.

But if you have the right skills, experience, and drive, you can get enough work to support yourself. You might not strike it rich, but you can make a living while loving what you do every day.

One of the roles that can make that life possible—and is very much in demand—is that of the graphic designer.

No matter what game you're playing, there was some element of graphic design necessary to create that game and turn it into a marketable product. Just recognize this isn't the same as art.

Graphic design is all about the layout, fonts, icons, and readability of the elements of a game. An artist, on the other hand, may be able to create amazing characters and worlds, but may not have the foggiest idea how to lay out a card and ensure bleed lines are properly employed.

3D modelers are a whole other category. They are the people who visualize, sculpt, and create figurines, commonly referred to as "minis" (as in mini figures). This is an even more highly specialized area of artistry.

I connected with a number of graphic artists to get a better understanding of how they got into the board game industry and make a living from what they do best.

DOI: 10.1201/9781003334408-13

Sebastian's Journey

Sebastian Koziner is a freelance graphic designer who also recently worked with IDW Games. He worked in the video game field for ten years before transitioning to tabletop games. He discovered he had a passion for creating user interfaces (UIs) and conveying information about the game to players. Over time, he discovered how to look at a game from both an artistic and commercial perspective, ensuring a game would become a good product as well as a fun experience.

Sebastian is quick to note that anyone can learn to use Photoshop and other programs, but these are only tools. There's so much more to it. Color theory, typography, morphology, and human psychology really come into play.

Sebastian goes on to say, "On the visual side, the first thing is to display information efficiently. To create a cohesive system of iconography and color that makes the information easy to understand to the user. Second to that is to make it look as beautiful as possible without sacrificing legibility, using all my artistic skills to make people not only [understand the game] but to enjoy their gaming."[21]

He is adamant that you have to think about the long game if you want to have a career in the creative fields, which include board games. He says the most important thing you need in any artistic service is a resume. He started by working on some small projects for new creators for very little money. Once he had about ten games on his resume, he started attracting the attention of some mid-sized publishers. It's all about building up your portfolio, getting better at what you do, and being OK with being paid very little at the start in order to attract bigger and better projects down the road. Sebastian says it's "…a marathon, and not a sprint."[21]

Sebastian says Boardgamegeek (BGG), which is the biggest social media site for board game lovers, was a lifesaver when he first started out. He now uses a combination of BGG and Facebook groups dedicated to games. Also, much of his work comes from companies he's worked with before. They love working together and have developed friendships, so there is no reason for these companies to look for someone else to work with. Repeat business is often the easiest to achieve.

You have to be willing to put yourself and your work out there for people to see. In Sebastian's words, "Create something. Don't wait on someone else to trust in you if you don't trust in yourself first, waiting in line for a chance to do something is the best way to do nothing." [21]

Matt Builds a Business Out of Graphic Design

Matt Paquette is one of the most in-demand names in graphic design within the board game industry. He was working full-time at a museum as a graphic & exhibition designer while freelancing on the side in the tabletop industry. In January 2018, he took the plunge and moved to tabletop full-time.

Matt says that the most important skills necessary to be successful as a freelance graphic designer in this industry are:

- "Creativity
- Eye for aesthetics
- Familiarity with the Adobe Creative Suite (since it's the industry standard)
- Ability to give and take creative direction"[22]

Matt built his reputation from word of mouth. He's tried the social media approach but admits he's not that good at it, so if this isn't your strong suit, take solace in the fact that social media is only one way to build your reputation. You can still find much success and work by simply being professional, working closely with publishers, and developing lasting relationships and a great reputation.

I should point out though that Matt is more than just a graphic designer. He is also the Creative Director of his own company. In addition, his agency helps with corporate strategy, creative and art direction, and a whole lot more.

Matt recommends first getting a taste for the industry by creating your own reference cards and other upgrades, picking up some small jobs here and there, and deciding whether this is the right role and industry for you before jumping in full-time with both feet. Being able to fill a need and creating a niche for yourself like he has is also a great way to go about this.[22]

Communication Is the Key

Hanna Björkman is also a freelance graphic designer and the owner of We Are Knytt, a full-service graphic design company that provides icons, illustrations, rulebook design and editing, and more.

While studying graphic design and communications at university, Hanna approached a board game publisher about creating a rulebook for them for a thesis. Being a lifelong board gamer, it was a natural transition to start a company and work as a freelancer in the industry.

Aside from knowledge of the Adobe suite of products and having an eye for detail, she says the ability to communicate with a client, understand what they want, and deliver are of the utmost importance. Clients often don't know what they want and don't have a lot of knowledge about graphic design, so it is often up to the graphic designer to help them understand what is needed and ensure players will easily understand how the game is played.

Hanna also started off small, doing work on prototypes and other small jobs to build a portfolio. Hanna is currently getting more active in various Facebook groups, sharing advice and insights, and has an Instagram account that analyzes already-published games. These methods showcase one's abilities and may attract future clients.

When asked about advice for someone trying to break into the industry as a graphic designer, Hanna shared, "As a freelancing graphic designer, it's hard. Most publishers have very tight margins, and they often don't have a lot of funds left for graphic design. I have several times gotten an answer about my quote along the lines of 'The price is completely fair, but we can't afford it.'"[23]

It's important to note that graphic design is a trained skill and most people working in graphic design have some formal education in the field. They also know the tools for the job, which are primarily the Adobe Suite, including Photoshop.

All these graphic designers shared that they may not make as much money working in a creative field like this as compared to a more corporate job, but what they get from it is flexibility and a job they love. So, if you've got graphic design skills, a strong work ethic, and value freedom, flexibility, and job satisfaction over money, being a freelance graphic designer in the board game industry might be a great fit for you.

Next, we'll look at the complementary role of artist and illustrator.

10

Artist/Illustrator

Most publishers also look to freelance artists for their games. Very few publishers will have full-time artists on staff.

It's important that we make the distinction between graphic designers and artists. A graphic designer is responsible for things like layout, fonts, iconography, and the general aesthetics and usability of the components in a game while an artist is responsible for the images used throughout. The artist creates the images that the graphic designer will arrange on the cards, boards, etc.

As a freelance artist, you may charge by the piece, by the hour, or give a rate for an entire project. Much depends on the publisher's budget. These rates can vary widely based on what is required, how much time is needed, and how many revisions must be made.

Combining Illustrations and Graphic Design

Tristam Rossin is an illustrator I deeply admire who also does a lot of graphic design work. On top of this, Tristam is a game designer and now a publisher as well. You could definitely say he is a "jack of all trades," and he somehow excels at all of them!

I hired Tristam as my illustrator and graphic designer for my solo campaign game, *Relics of Rajavihara,* after seeing his amazing work on other projects and hearing other creators speak so favorably about him.

Prior to joining the board game world, Tristam worked for twenty years doing commercial design and illustration, mostly in the education sector. After his job was made redundant, he turned to his hobby of game design

DOI: 10.1201/9781003334408-14

and set out to use his existing skills and experience to create a career in an exciting new field.

One of the things I love about Tristam is how involved he is in the game design community. He's very active in several game design Facebook groups, always asking for feedback on his latest illustrations and taking those suggestions to make helpful improvements. He also gives back by sharing his thoughts and expertise when others pose questions about their own games.

It's through posting and sharing his work in these groups that he has built a following. When one of his games is released (either self-published or through another publisher), people know a lot about it already, having seen it developed from the early stages. This also leads to many creators reaching out to ask him to work on their projects. He doesn't need to advertise his services, as people come to him!

However, it's not all fun and games.

Tristam admits that he often works six or seven days a week, twelve hours a day. He loves what he does, so it doesn't often feel like work, but he says it can become all-consuming trying to make a good living in the industry.

However, he now has the ability to choose what projects he works on and is often booked months in advance. This goes to show how important it is to put your art out there and get it in front of people. They will see what you're capable of, as well as how you take feedback and use it to improve what you've already created. It shows that you can take direction and that you're easy to work with.

Tristam's advice? "Join the Facebook groups, get involved, help others, become part of the community. Don't hide your work and show it in the last steps of development, get it out there from day one, listen to the criticisms, and be humble in your approach…"[24]

Many people, whether they are game designers or artists, worry about having their ideas stolen. However, the board game industry is a small community where most people know each other. It is very rare for an idea to be stolen, and even if it is, it is the actual execution of the idea that is the most important. Besides, most people are excited about their own game ideas and don't have as much time or interest in the ideas of others.

Again, diversification can greatly help you in the industry. If you don't have any projects lined up in one area, there may be others waiting for you elsewhere. Or, you can be working on your own game or preparing to self-publish a game.

Having multiple streams of income can definitely help level out the highs and lows in generating income that often comes with working in the industry.

Non-Starving Artists

Beth Sobel is another artist who has already made a name for herself. She is the illustrator behind games like *Wingspan, Calico,* and *Lord of the Rings: The Card Game.*

Beth went to graduate school for oil painting and completed her Master of Fine Arts (MFA), but got into board games by chance. She got hired to do some card art for a publisher, as well as her first full board game in 2013, Jamey Stegmaier's *Viticulture.*

While her experience was more in oil painting, she quickly discovered that you need more flexibility when editing, so she now draws and paints digitally. Beth loves being given direction on what a creator is looking for and then bringing this to life in her art.[25]

Kwanchai Moriya is another well-known illustrator in the board game world, who has worked with board game publishers like Haba Games, Pandasaurus Games, Funko Games, and Renegade Game Studios.

In addition to illustrations, Kwanchai also does graphic design and logo work.

Early on, he was quite active on BGG, doing his own fan art redesigns. A few publishers reached out to him to offer him gigs doing illustrations for their upcoming games, including Ezra's *Catacombs* 3rd edition.

Kwanchai started attending many board game conventions in 2010, showing his portfolio to as many publishers as he could meet with, usually landing at least a few gigs. He admits "With my scant experience, publishers were apt to pay very little and over direct a project to death. Definitely a lot of stress in those early years was because I was learning the business side of freelancing on the go, while butchering my work/life balance, and flexing relatively weak artistic muscles."[26]

Now that he has a lot more experience and has become well-known, publishers often come to him! Kwanchai says "With my clients now, there's more trust that I can get a project wrapped on time and it can look good. Earlier projects did tend to be over-directed, with a lot of hand-holding. But I don't blame publishers, as choosing an artist is one of the many risks they take on in the process of making a game." [26]

But this does pose challenges, as he's often asked to work on a game in a completely different style than his past projects and people have high expectations (as does he for himself), which he admits can be very stressful. "The negative side of an increased reputation is an increased expectation from people. Or perhaps I have an increased expectation that other people have an increased expectation? For sure I'm harder on myself now, and more scared to make mistakes. I feel like I have to constantly hit home runs, even though I just learned how to play."[26]

Kwanchai is quick to admit that it was a long, winding path getting to where he is today. This included amassing a lot of student debt and taking years to find his direction and build a reputation. So, don't be discouraged if you're not an overnight success! Kwanchai suggests "Explore a multitude of paths, and work whatever side jobs you need to. But when it's go-time, make the jump and bring all your time and resources to bear."[26]

Vincent Dutrait is another accomplished artist in the board game industry. He is known for his work on *Tikal II, Lewis & Clark, Rising 5*, and *Time Stories,* among many other games. Most of Vincent's prior work was in children's books, including *La Balafre* and *Le Prince Des Nuages*, then in 2010 he contacted some board game publishers and landed his first gigs in the industry.

Vincent only works in traditional mediums, then scans his images and does the final color corrections. He considers this his "trademark." He says "Some commissions are simply a summarized list of images to create, without any consultation from me. That's fine, but it is often frustrating and not all that constructive. I greatly prefer to share, discuss, and participate in the development of the game."[27]

He spends a lot of time researching and thinking about the art piece rather than making rough sketches. This can take up to two-thirds of the time in creating an illustration.

Vincent feels that "a game is a whole package, made of mechanics, theme, images, and players. I find it much more complex and nebulous as compared to illustrating a book. Additionally, players are more and more demanding, fussy, and attentive to what is offered. It is a formidable challenge that leaves little room for amateurism."[27]

This goes to show how important it is to be professional and deliver a great product within timelines and budget. You have to be able to adapt to different styles and work with individuals who have different needs and working methods. Plus, you have to create art that is beautiful, functional, and in line with the game.

It can be a long road, working on many low-paying projects to build up your expertise and reputation. Many will give up along the way, but those who work hard, develop strong connections and build their reputation as a great artist and someone who is fantastic to work with *can* make a living creating amazing works of art in the board game world.

11

Writer/Editor
(or Rulebook Creator)

If you're good with words, board game publishers need you!

There are two different writing styles we're going to get into here that are very distinct: fictional writing and technical writing.

In this chapter, we'll be looking at both of these writing styles and where each one fits into the board game world.

Fictional Writing

If you're good at fictional writing—that is, writing about characters, worlds, lore, and backstories—you might be able to find a place for yourself helping publishers bring the stories in their games to life.

This is likely going to be the harder route of the two, as it is less in demand. Every game needs a rulebook that is easy to understand, but not every game needs a lot of story behind it. Story-based games and role-playing games (RPGs) are the main types of games where fictional writing is needed.

Nikki Valens was a Senior Game Designer at Fantasy Flight Games (FFG) from 2013 to 2018. Some of her credits include *Arkham Horror* and *Mansions of Madness*. She is drawn to co-op games, particularly narrative-driven ones, and likes to add a lot of character and story to the games she works on.

Nikki landed the job at FFG by simply applying to an open position. However, she had done work on RPGs in the past, which also got their attention and let them know that she was good at writing and building worlds and stories into games.

DOI: 10.1201/9781003334408-15

Nikki notes that one of the challenges of creating a narrative game is that you want to be able to tell a story, but still allow players to make their own choices and discover different parts of the world. It's like a *Choose Your Own Adventure* book. You have to create all these paths that players can take and leave it up to them to determine how to play and what they want to do. When asked about how she went about creating her game, *Legacy of Dragonholt*, Nikki said "The system itself is so light, that it only took a few days and a couple tests to know I had landed on something I liked. But the sheer amount of narrative that exists in the game took a long while to produce."[28]

It should be noted that while Nikki did write for RPGs in her earlier days, her current projects involve the design, development, and narrative for these games, not just the writing alone.

It's definitely a niche within the industry. Quite often, it will be the game designers or developers themselves who write the story behind their games, but you might be able to find some freelance gigs here and there if you can prove to others that you can write well and tell a great story that a creator can include in their game.

In reality, if you're an author, writing stories for board games may just be one small part of your income. You'll likely write books or do work in other industries as well.

Because many game designers do their own story writing, the real demand in the industry, when it comes to writing, is for those who are really good at technical writing and can create a rulebook that is easily understood by players.

Rulebook Writing and Editing

Every game needs a rulebook. There are no exceptions.

Some only need very simple, one-page instructions, while others require dozens of pages to explain in great detail all the various parts of a game.

This is where technical writing and editing expertise really comes into play.

Dustin Schwartz was the first person I had ever heard of who was a dedicated rulebook editor when I discovered him on the Board Game Design Lab Podcast. He offers proofreading and copyediting services.

His proofreading service is intended for rulebooks that have already been edited and include looking for typos, punctuation and spelling mistakes, bad grammar, and inconsistencies.

Copyediting goes a step further. This is where Dustin looks over a rule-book for structure, style, voice, and layout.

Dustin has done rulebook editing for many publishers over the years, including Foxtrot Games, Thunderworks Games, Renegade Game Studios, IDW, and Restoration Games.

One look at his portfolio and you can see that he relies on working with many of the same publishers, game after game. That's what can come from showing one company that you're really good at what you do and that you deliver great results on schedule.

In fact, Dustin has edited at least five game rulebooks for each of eight different companies. Renegade Game Studios has hired him an astonishing thirty-four times! Now that's a lot of repeat business. It's much easier to find work with companies you have worked with before by delivering solid results. They are much more likely to come back to you rather than roll the dice on an unknown contractor.[29]

Dustin has been able to build his portfolio and list of clients through word of mouth, as well as appearances on podcasts—like the Board Game Design Lab podcast—and interviews talking about rulebook editing.

However, when you can combine editing, design, and layout, you've got an even more compelling package you can offer a publisher.

Full Rulebook Design

My friend Jeff Fraser, whom I mentioned previously, was working in journal-ism but decided to leave the field in 2017 to pursue a career in the board game industry. Initially, he wanted to be a game designer, but he wasn't finding suc-cess in getting his games signed with publishers. However, he was able to make a lot of contacts within the industry and realized he had an opportunity to pivot.

Jeff's Master's Degree in Journalism and experience in the field, along with strong graphic design skills, put him in a great position to become a freelance rulebook editor. He is not only able to edit a rulebook extremely well, but also understands layout and graphic design, so he can offer all these services in one great package.

With a resume that now includes work he's done with Pandasaurus Games, WizKids, Academy Games, and Everything Epic, he's also becoming recog-nized as a strong game developer.

When asked what skills are the most important to be successful in his role, Jeff listed, "Strong command of English grammar and style rules, the ability to break down complex concepts in plain English, the ability to hit tight deadlines, the ability to juggle lots of different projects at once, and teamwork."[30]

Jeff says that he was able to build his reputation by finding a poorly served but much-needed niche, and convincing publishers that his experience was very relevant to rulebook editing. He charged a lower rate when he first started so he could get his foot in the door, and then was able to raise his rates once he had more experience and connections.

Isn't this sounding like a common thread among so many of these jobs? I mentioned this in the introduction, and you've seen this pattern time and time again throughout the book—building up a reputation through volunteering or lower playing work, then becoming much more in demand.

Jeff, like many others, finds most of his work through word of mouth. Jeff also attends a lot of tabletop conventions and events, where he has the opportunity to meet with decision-makers at different publishers relatively easily.

He notes that most people in the industry are wonderful creative types; however, few are experienced in project management and creative direction, and many freelancers do this as a side gig. The downside to taking on a role like this is that it can sometimes lead to chaos, disorganization, inconsistency, and frustration.

When asked about other entry-level roles in the industry people might consider, Jeff says "Customer service, project management, logistics, sales, and any business-side expertise are all very sought after. Some folks have found more stable jobs in publishing-adjacent businesses, like game manufacturing or fulfilment and shipping."[30]

Many of these opportunities in adjacent and related industries that he mentioned here are well worth considering for the added stability and security and will be discussed in the next chapter.

Section IV

Everything You Wanted to Know about Other Roles but were Too Afraid to Ask

12

Help Games Get to Customers

Designers make games. Developers take them that last mile over the finish line. Publishers commission art and design, then put everything together.

But have you ever thought about how games are physically made? How do they get into stores? How do customers find and purchase their next favorite game?

There are many steps in this cycle, and we'll look at all of them in this chapter, revealing all the job opportunities that exist throughout this process.

Manufacturing

Games have to be physically created before people can enjoy them. That's where manufacturing comes in. This is mostly done in China, but there are other countries where the infrastructure exists and games are manufactured as well.

I spoke with Shero Li, Project Manager at Magicraft, the company that is manufacturing my game, *Relics of Rajavihara*, about her experience.

Shero says her main responsibility is to help to bring her client's ideas to life. It is a balancing act that she tries to get right for every client. Shero says she has been successful because she "…will provide professional suggestions to my clients and help them to balance the cost and quality of the board game."[31] Different problems sometimes arise, so she has to be able to deal with these quickly and professionally. Each detail has to be just right to make a great game.

Since every detail has to be so precise, it is helpful to have a good amount of experience both with board games and in manufacturing.

DOI: 10.1201/9781003334408-17

She recommends looking for posted positions and networking with others you know if you are interested in finding a job in the world of board game manufacturing. But if you don't live near a board game manufacturer and aren't interested in moving halfway around the world, there are still opportunities to work for manufacturers in other roles.[31]

Kerry Rundle and Sarah Graybill are both Project Managers at Panda Game Manufacturing, a company recognized for its high quality. One of the things they offer that most other manufacturers don't have is a project manager who speaks the same language as most creators, thereby reducing communication barriers.

Kerry and Sarah both work in the US, despite the fact that their company manufactures everything in China. Much like Shero, they work directly with clients to bring their games to life. They have to balance costs, quality, and timelines. They also love finding ways to add little things to the game for stretch goals and bonuses that add a lot of perceived value without a lot more cost. For example, UV spot finish on the box top, improved card quality, and custom wood components.[32]

Working as project managers in the board game industry, they spend most of their time communicating with clients and potential clients, answering questions, providing quotes, and ensuring projects are completed on time and on budget.

So, while the opportunities to project manage from home might be in short supply, they are out there if you know where to look.

However, there are still other positions that you might want to consider as well.

Sales for Manufacturers

I met Dave Snyder at Protospiel Michigan a couple of years ago. He works for Gameland, another manufacturer in China. His role is US Director of Sales.

Dave was working part-time as a sales associate for one game manufacturer and was considering transitioning to full-time in the industry. This worked out well, as Gameland was looking for a US representative at this very same time. He was also making metal dice within the gaming industry (and continues to do so), so he balances his time between working for Gameland full-time, making dice, and doing work in the plastic injection industry (he is semi-retired as a mold maker and tooling engineer).

While Dave does have manufacturing and engineering degrees and acknowledges they are helpful for him, he doesn't feel they are a necessity for his current role. While he says skills are needed, without the qualities of enthusiasm, honesty, and commitment, he wouldn't be nearly as effective as he is. People remember this and return to him when they have questions or want to find a partner to work with to manufacture their game.

Dave attends a lot of industry events, including Protospiels (game design retreats) and conventions. He says that when he attends these events and meets new people, his main responsibilities are to "Introduce people to our company and emphasize that we are their best choice for their project—and also be able to honestly advise them when we are not."[33]

Like many others I connected with, he emphasizes that you sometimes need to take some sort of role in the industry for little or no money, just to get your foot in the door. Helping others by referring his dice customers to another manufacturer was his first step and got him some part-time work in the industry, which led to the full-time role he has now.

It's not easy though. Dave admits he doesn't earn a ton of money and it is definitely less than what he made in his previous occupation, but he is far happier and healthier than he was before. He explains how he is able to make this happen:

> I have five things that allowed me to pursue this as a 'full time' operation:
>
> 1. No debt
> 2. Emergency income for two years
> 3. Health benefits through my spouse
> 4. Backup income sources (mold making and dice business)
> 5. I maintain a fairly frugal lifestyle[33]

He suggests that if you don't have at least three of these boxes checked off, start by finding something part-time or on the side before considering going full-time.

Dave reminds us that it is a marathon, not a sprint. He suggests trying to get your foot in the door in a part of the industry that interests you and set a goal to make this more permanent two to three years from now. It may take more time or it may take less time, but he says you need to be prepared for this to not happen overnight and be OK with that.[33]

Shipping and Fulfillment

Once a game has been manufactured, it needs to be shipped around the world to stores, backers, and anyone else who purchased your game. That's where shipping and fulfillment come in.

Jon Homfray works for the shipping, fulfillment, and distribution company Spiral Galaxy. He's based in the UK and will be handling the fulfillment of my game, *Relics of Rajavihara,* for many parts of the world, including the EU.

Jon is Spiral Galaxy's Fulfillment/Project Coordinator. He started out in their sister company, Gameslore, with the dispatch and warehousing team, then moved into his role at Spiral Galaxy when a position became available. It was a formal process for getting into the initial role, as well as the promotion.

Jon lists his primary responsibilities as:

- Seeking out and retaining new publishers and clients
- The primary point of contact for planning, problem-solving, and ongoing relations
- Managing the import, manipulation, and maintaining of data for publishers
- Problem solving for publishers, manufacturers, and end customers
- Organizing and handling import and export of freight
- Overseeing the dispatch and customer support teams
- Other assorted tasks[34]

As many others have said, the key skills required in his role include communication skills, networking and interpersonal skills, organization, and a good work ethic.

When asked about the realities of his job that he hadn't anticipated, Jon replied, "The level of stress involved. We are a growing company in a niche market and as such we must be flexible and take on more individual work than might be required in other industries. It can be quite overwhelming! Also you would imagine that working in the board game industry you would get to play a great deal of board games; unfortunately, I have found much the opposite!" [34]

However, he loves the flexibility, ability to go to conventions and meet amazing people, and working with publishers he admires. For him, the trade-off is worth it.

Jon's advice for anyone looking to work in the game industry: "Get to know people in the industry and be prepared to get your feet wet! While knowing the right people won't automatically open doors it will certainly present opportunities. You need to take these opportunities when they arise and run with them. Once in the industry, you can continue to grow and open other doors."[34]

Tyler Smith is also in the shipping/fulfillment/distribution game. He runs D6, which is based in North America, and ships within the continent and beyond.

He has very similar responsibilities to Jon; however, he runs his own company, so he's even more accountable for everything that goes on.

Tyler admits that much of his day involves looking at spreadsheets. It's all about costs, logistics, and getting the games delivered on time and on budget.

He also does many personal calls with current and potential clients, ensuring that they understand all the steps in the process. His expertise and positive word-of-mouth feedback are what get him a steady flow of clients.[35]

It must be noted that the shipping and fulfillment side creates a very busy life. It never stops. Packages are always coming in that need to be delivered. Delays happen that are out of your control. You have to be able to solve all the problems that come up regularly. It's not for the faint of heart!

However, there are still other stops to consider between getting a game manufactured and getting it into a customer's hands.

Retail (Board Game Stores)

AJ Brandon is the Storefront Manager at Board Game Bliss, one of my favorite friendly local game stores (FLGS). Board Game Bliss was his favorite store and he followed them on Facebook, where he saw they were hiring. He applied, went through an interview, and the rest, as they say, is history.

He held a variety of jobs prior to working in this retail board game store, but his management experience in another retail sector, along with his love of board games, and the store itself, was what got him the position.

As expected in a retail position, customer service, interpersonal communication, politeness, and professionalism are the skills that will land you the job and help you to excel in the role.

AJ says his main responsibilities are to "keep the store clean and organized, manage used games, greet customers and find them games/give recommendations, run math trades, organize other events, teach demo games, and answer emails pertaining to my work."[36]

He says that the pay isn't fantastic and it is certainly less than many other industries, but it can also pay decently compared to other retail jobs, depending on the store. An obvious entry-level position would be retail associate, which could lead to a management position with hard work and experience.

AJ has become well known in the community for his welcoming style, community building, and ability to give great game recommendations. In fact, he's becoming more well-known across the industry for the talks he's given to designers and publishers on creating a great retail experience.[36]

He now co-hosts the podcast Fun Problems with Peter C. Hayward, and is getting consulting gigs to help clients design box covers that will get attention—and he doesn't even need to advertise!

This goes to show that if you put in the time and work hard, it's possible to be seen as an expert in your area and people will start coming to you for advice. This can lead to consulting work and other opportunities for you down the road.

Board Game Cafés

Another similar avenue that you might consider is that of board game cafés. These are wonderful places that allow people to have a drink, meal, or snacks, all while playing a bunch of new and favorite board games with friends.

There are lots of potential positions available at board game cafés, from owner to manager to server to game guru (an individual who teaches games to patrons).

Snakes & Lattes is a board game café that now has multiple locations in Toronto and has also expanded to Phoenix. There is almost always a game guru on staff to teach games or refresh the rules for players. It is quite an undertaking to learn, remember, and be a good teacher of rules for dozens or even hundreds of games, but if this is something you're good at, it may be a great fit for you!

Board game stores and cafes are prevalent in many places around the world, especially in big cities. There are at least a half dozen in Toronto alone! You just need to look around to see who is hiring. You may also be thinking of opening up a board game café yourself! If you do, remember that you will be essentially opening up a restaurant that also offers games to play. The collection of games has to be good, but so does the food and drink.

Opening or working in a board game café might just be the first step you need to get your foot in the door in the industry.

13

Marketing, Consulting, and Video Production

Another approach you could consider is helping game designers and publishers to get the word out. This can be done through multiple channels, including marketing, consulting, or video production.

Let's take a look at what each of these entails.

Marketing

Coming up with an awesome game is the easy part. Well, it's not that easy, but in many ways, it is easier to create the game than to market it well, find your audience, and generate a good number of sales.

This is an area where many creators struggle. They are great with the creative side but on the marketing and promotion side? Not so much.

We see so many creative types enter the space, but few, who are entrepreneurs or who really understand the selling side of things. We have many dreamers, but very few MBAs.

There is definitely a gap here that needs to be filled.

I spoke with one of the most knowledgeable people in the board game marketing space about how they have been able to find their niche in the industry.

Nalin Chuapetcharasopon runs Crush Crowdfunding (crushcrowdfunding.com) and Meeple Marketing (meeplemarketing.com).

DOI: 10.1201/9781003334408-18

I asked how she found herself in her position—I'll let her tell the whole fascinating story in her own words:

> "I'm a marketer by trade and have been in the crowdfunding space since 2015. In 2020, I noticed on Google Analytics that one particular article on my blog about launching board games was getting a lot of hits.
>
> "Since I already play a lot of tabletop games with my wife and have the marketing and crowdfunding experience, I started looking at what was out there to help game designers launch their ideas.
>
> "During that time, I devoured as much content as possible including Jamey Stegmaier's book and blogs as well as that from James Mathe. Since the content hasn't been updated, my curiosity took me down a rabbit hole where I started looking at different places to see how game designers are figuring out how to market their games for Kickstarter.
>
> "This essentially made me realize that people are looking for and need a lot of help in this area. I asked people what they wanted to learn more about and started writing marketing and crowdfunding blogs, as well as posting content about marketing. Game designers continued to enjoy the content and find value from it, so I kept going. This spiraled into what it is today—a blog, podcast, and community for games designers looking to market their games for Kickstarter."[37]

That's how you do it. You find something that is missing and that people need help with, and you provide value and help them to solve their problems. This builds your reputation and people reach out to work with you.

Nalin says the most important skill in her role is consistency. I would highly agree with this. When people see you show up every day and provide great content, they can't help but notice you.

She says, it is incredibly important to understand marketing in her role. How to market yourself, your products, and how to find your audience.

Nalin suggests that anyone interested in getting into the board game industry should start by "doing." Learn the skills and show off what you can do. Start with the lens of helping others and good things will follow.

If you're looking to get into board game marketing specifically, she suggests getting started by working on social media pages, doing hashtag research, creating images, and writing copy.

Nalin isn't able to run Meeple Marketing full-time yet, but she makes a decent living through her role in the general crowdfunding market. She intends to grow her business through consulting, marketing, and content.

Once again, we see an approach that is looking at multiple potential streams of income.

Nalin's skills are very transferable and there will always be a need for marketing in board games (as well as in any other industry). However, when it comes to marketing *herself*, she doesn't really need to, as she has people reaching out to her for help.[37]

This is what happens when you provide great content and show that you know your stuff. People naturally want to work with you!

Consulting

Brandon Rollins runs Pangea Games as well as the Pangea Marketing Agency. It was his website and blogs about creating your first game and all the things he wished he knew when he first started out that led to him developing a strong following. People began reaching out to him for marketing advice, and he ended up doing so much consulting that he started his agency, which has become much more of his focus than his original focus of making games.

Brandon says one trait is more important than all others. "I could make a case for a lot of different skills, but the mother of all of them is patience. If you want to make a board game or start a company, it's going to inevitably involve a ton of trial and error. Patience will keep your ears open when someone needs to tell you something you need to hear but don't want to. Patience will keep you going for long enough for you to reap the fruits of labor."[38]

Brandon has blogged about his experiences every week for five years straight. His consistency and helpful advice helped him build trust with his audience, with individuals looking to get their games to market, and with search engines, which allowed him to reach even more people.

He offers free consultations with creators, which is a great way to help others build their trust in him and works very well in the long term. As a result, he's able to work closely with a small number of clients, while picking up occasional one-off consults.

The great thing about providing so much valuable content is that much like Nalin, Brandon doesn't need to advertise. People come to him through his blogs and referrals.

Brandon relates how creating a game on your own allows you to learn a lot. He says "board game design taught me: graphic design, supply chain management, market research, event planning, and more."[38]

Still, he recommends a cautious approach. "Try it on the side first. While it's extra work, the benefit of this, in addition to extra money, is that you can build contacts, figure out if you really like the industry, and find other things you're passionate about…all without the risk of, say, quitting your job outright."[38]

While marketing is one definite area where you can do consulting, there are other areas as well.

You could be a consultant in the retail space, like AJ Brandon mentioned in a previous chapter.

You could also consult on Kickstarter campaigns, either on the marketing side or in other areas, advising creators on how to structure their campaign page, set pledge levels, and determine their funding goal.

Anywhere you see a need, if you have the skills and expertise, see if you can fill that gap as a consultant!

Video Production

Literally thousands of board game Kickstarter campaigns launch every year. It's no longer the case that you can just put up a video of your idea and hope that people will support you.

Nowadays, you're competing with some big names in the industry. Since the most successful campaigns have a great video, there's a growing need for people who understand what it takes to make a compelling video that will get the attention of potential backers. These videos are sometimes animated, sometimes live, and sometimes a combination of the two. They may use 2D or 3D visuals.

Ori Kagan is the Founder and Project Manager behind Kagan Productions. After working for ten years as an editor/animator, he realized that working in a studio for someone else wasn't for him. So, he decided to go freelance.

After working on several projects, he decided to combine two things he loved—animation and board games. He started small by reaching out to local game designers in Israel and offering to create animated Kickstarter videos. He offered them at a very modest budget so he could create a portfolio.

He then created a website to share his videos. Word of mouth got out and more projects came to him from other board game creators. He's never had to do any sort of paid marketing. Ori's clients recommend him to others frequently, so he never has a shortage of projects on the go.

Ori's BA in film studies and experience working for a studio gave him the skills he needed to run the whole show, including production management, going from script to final product, and, of course, animating the videos—both in 2D and 3D.

When it comes to getting a start as a video producer, Ori's advice is to "create a strong portfolio, take jobs for a low budget, and make something that would cost triple that or more."[39]

It's all about over-delivering on what you promised. Clients will realize they got great value and will not only come back time and time again, but they will also tell everyone they know!

David Diaz also makes Kickstarter videos for creators. He is the founder and Creative Director at Mesa Game Lab.

His story of getting into video animation is quite different. He's also a game designer, and after he signed his first game, *Fossilis*, David decided to create some animated GIFs for the publisher with the help of two friends. Having worked in the animation industry for fifteen years, it was no sweat to make this contribution, which he knew would benefit the campaign.

He received such great feedback that they decided to make this a side business, and Mesa Game Lab was born.

David's experience as a game designer, along with the fact that he has backed many games on Kickstarter and knows what backers want to see, also helps him on the animation side.

David is not naturally drawn to social media, but he has had to embrace it more recently. By being part of many Facebook groups and posting about the projects he's working on here and on a couple of other social media platforms, as well as YouTube and their own website, David has found many clients.

He's also planning on sponsoring Tantrum House's "Games Coming to Kickstarter" videos and hopes this will drive even more business his way.

David's advice for anyone serious about getting into the industry is: "Firstly, play a lot of games! The more you know about the industry the better. And secondly, get to know people in the industry. Attend local gaming events and others further away, if you can. Introduce yourself to as many designers and publishers as you can so they get to know your name and face and expand that on social media. Make yourself available to help others test their games so others will be more likely to help you when you need it."[40]

Once again, getting to know others in the industry and putting yourself out there for others to see your amazing work are crucial steps on the way to turning a side business into something full-time. Offering a helping hand also goes a long way.

If you make great videos, show them off! Wow, other creators and make sure it's easy for them to find you.

In the next chapter, we'll look at other forms of content creation that can lead to fulfilling work as well.

14

Content Creation

With thousands of new games coming out every year via Kickstarter, conventions, and retail releases, there is so much to be covered. But there's plenty of other content related to games, game design, and plenty of other topics also being created and consumed.

In this chapter, we'll look at several different types of content creation, including an inside look at many amazing content creators and how you can find your own niche.

Building a Community

There's a lot of great game design content out there for aspiring game designers, like James Mathe's website and Jamey Stegmaier's Kickstarter Lessons blog and Crowdfunding Guide.

Many creators have found a lot of fulfillment in providing helpful advice and lessons learned to others, and a byproduct of this has been a larger audience, along with gaining trust.

Gabe Barrett runs the Board Game Design Lab (BGDL). It began as a humble podcast and has grown into something much larger. He now also runs a very active Facebook community with over eight thousand members and has multiple game-design-related books, calendars, and a starter kit to help game designers get started quickly.

Gabe says that the reason he started the BGDL was that he couldn't find the game design resources or content he wanted and needed, so he set out to create this himself.

DOI: 10.1201/9781003334408-19

Once again, we see someone noticing a gap and doing what they can to fill it.

Gabe says the key to success for him has been through helpfulness, focus, and consistency. He has released a new podcast every single week for over two hundred weeks straight. Showing up consistently definitely brings you a lot of attention.

It should be noted that along with managing all the aspects of the BGDL community and podcast, Gabe also designs and publishes his own games, as well as writing and publishing his own books on game design.

Gabe notes, as many others do, "The business side of things takes *waaay* more of my time than I expected. That's a common thing I hear people say about getting into publishing full time, and it's absolutely correct."[41] However, hearing from others how his podcast and community has helped them through bouts of depression, losing a loved one, and other major life events makes it all worthwhile.

When asked how someone could get started in the industry, Gabe emphasized, "Volunteer. Whether it's to be a playtester or to help a company out at a convention, get your foot in the door by showing people you're dependable and a pleasure to work with. All industries are relationship based, but the gaming industry is especially so. So, build relationships."[41]

As you get further into the industry, he suggests looking for ways to create multiple streams of income, so that when one stream is dry (ex: no royalty payments are coming in), you still have other income (ex: book sales, game development, etc.).

He also suggests ways to save money to do what you love, such as, "If you live in an area where the cost of living is really high, I encourage you to think through if moving to a cheaper area would help you better accomplish your goals. If you can drop your living expenses by 10 percent, you could redirect that money into other things or maybe even take a job you love that comes with a pay cut."[41]

When I asked Gabe what his advice would be for anyone looking to work in the industry, he said, "There's no such thing as a dream job, and every job comes with its fair share of things that are great and things that are annoying and even downright terrible. Make sure your eyes are completely open to the reality of what any job in any industry really is.

"If you want to work in the gaming industry, go for it, but be careful not to put it on a pedestal, as you'll be sorely disappointed. However, with all the good, bad, and ugly I've experienced, I've greatly enjoyed my time."[41]

Who Says Magazines Have to Be Printed?

Cameron Art is at an earlier stage than Gabe. He runs Cameron Art Games, which is a side business, and he produces the *Board Game Bulletin (BGB)*, which is a monthly collection of interviews, videos, articles, and images, all related to board games.

Cameron designed games for fun, but it wasn't until he stumbled upon Jamey Stegmaier's blog that he decided he wanted to release a game of his own. That game was called Vowl. It didn't achieve its funding goals on its first run on Kickstarter, but Cameron learned a lot from the experience and is relaunching it with his newfound knowledge.

But Cameron also wanted to contribute and give back to the community. He says, "There have been various tabletop game magazines that have released over the years, but most of them have died off fairly quickly (with a few exceptions), and almost none of them are completely free to read. I wanted something that was easily accessible to anyone who wanted to read it and that featured a wide variety of different content, not just written articles. That's how The BGB came to exist in its current state: an online, interactive magazine that is always free."[42]

He isn't earning much from the *Board Game Bulletin* yet, but what he does earn he smartly reinvests in his business and himself. He highlights the need for strong communication and project management skills to create consistent content, especially when you must coordinate with four to five other contributors.

Cameron shared his advice for those looking to break into the industry: "Unless you have a job offer or the relevant skills to apply for a job, don't get serious about 'making' a career. Working for yourself is hard enough, but making a living working for yourself is even harder. It's not easy to find jobs with an easily livable income in the board gaming hobby. But, I am a firm believer that people should always try to do what they love, even if it means living frugally, rather than doing something you hate that makes a lot of money. If you love what you do, you'll never work a day in your life."[42]

Blogging Builds a Following

Brandon Rollins, who was mentioned in a previous chapter is another great content creator who consistently puts out helpful, quality content every single week. This has led him to gather a following of over two thousand people on his weekly newsletter, as well as a large Discord group (which is like a meeting place for people to chat over text and voice, used frequently in the gaming community).[38]

I have been blogging weekly for over two-and-a-half years myself, providing tips and stories about my own game design experiences. At first, I had very few people reading, but now I have over two thousand subscribers, along with thousands of views on my website every month.

Aspiring game designers can come to my site and see that I have a wealth of information freely available to them. They can see the quality of the content and the interesting topics that I tackle. This builds trust.

Imagine if I had quit blogging and building my email list after three months, when next to nobody was reading what I had to say? I wouldn't have built the following I have now, and not nearly as many people would have trusted me enough to buy the books I've written or take the courses I have created.

Yes, it is a lot of work. Yes, it can be hard. Success won't happen overnight. It's going to take time. But when you make consistency a habit, you will start to see results. It's important not to give up if you don't see the needle moving quickly enough right off the bat.

Give it some time and keep doing what you're doing, honing your skills, and improving on what you do. The added benefit is that fewer people will see your earlier videos and posts where you were still figuring out camera angles, lighting, what content you wanted to focus on, or your writing style. Make these mistakes early and learn from them.

It's not just the content, though. Most content creators do other things and have multiple streams of income, whether they consult, design games, publish games, write books, or offer other products and services. Diversification is good!

It's all about finding ways to get into the industry that match well with your passions, skills, and experience. Then do that one thing consistently, and get better at it over time. Once you have some success in one area, you can branch out in another direction and build on your successes.

Game Reviews and Previews

Mark Maia has been working in the video game industry for twenty-one years but has turned his attention to tabletop games in the past few years. He and his wife, Brittany, are the founders of Board Game Coffee, a popular board game review channel.

Brittany wanted to start a website related to board games, but it conflicted with her day job. At the same time, Mark was working on designing a game of his own. Brittany suggested creating a board game channel and asked Mark to host. He was hesitant, but eventually gave in when he realized he needed to get involved in the community in some way if he ever wanted to kickstart his own game. So, Board Game Coffee was born!

As a reviewer, Mark is responsible for writing their scripts, hosting most of the episodes, and editing the videos, along with teaching the games to others on the team. Brittany is usually behind the camera but sometimes makes guest appearances. She handles a lot of the behind-the-scenes tasks as well.

Mark says "Be honest, be confident, love what you do, and don't take life too seriously. I also look at everything as a challenge to overcome, which is good in some ways because it pushes you to better yourself, but to be honest is a little stressful so that's something I have to work on myself. Oh… and be personable, people are the most important thing in this industry."[43]

He is focused on constantly improving himself and wants to be recognized for his work rather than getting attention on himself, which was what made him hesitant about starting the channel, to begin with.

While it is a fun job, he recognizes it is still a job. Sure, he gets to play a lot of games and receives many of them for free, but "It's more work than I had anticipated. Learning games and editing video to meet deadlines, and to get stuff out before the other guy is stressful."[43] He and Brittany both have daytime jobs as well, so this is something they do on the side.

Mark says if you want to get into the industry, look for internships or playtester roles. However, if you want to be a reviewer or create other content, "just turn on your phone and get to work."[43]

At first, they had to reach out to publishers for games to review, but when they started to get recognized for their quality content, publishers started reaching out to them. Mark confides, "If you're going into board game media, know that it's going to be hard and a lot of work for a long time. Be ready for that."[43]

The barrier to entry for board game media is very low. Anyone with a phone and a few games can become a reviewer. But if you want to do this long term, you need to do something that makes you stand out from the rest and gets people coming back to consume your content. It might be your style, the types of games you review, or something else that sets you apart. You also have to be consistent and keep putting out great quality content all the time.

Mark says that it's the people that keep him going. If it weren't for all the amazing people in the industry and friends he's met along the way, he wouldn't still be doing this. He admits," If it wasn't for the people, I'd probably drop out."[43] It's a lot of hard work, and you can't be afraid to fail, as that's where you'll learn the most.

Note that content and video creation can incorporate more than just reviews—you could create previews (overview), unboxing videos, playthroughs, how–to-play/rules videos, written reviews, and so much more.

Self-Taught

Jesse Samuel Anderson is another rising star in the board game media world. He runs the Quackalope channel, which also reviews games, and takes more of a cinematic approach to game previews.

Jesse says, "I have always been an entrepreneur from self-publishing a book at 14 to wedding photography after college. I do what I enjoy, build a career around the pursuit, and always try to grow, learn, and improve myself."[44]

He enjoys the freedom of doing what he wants and working on projects he enjoys. He says he would never trade this for a nine-to-five desk job.

Almost everything he's learned has been self-taught. He does everything himself at his company. He enjoys working with others and loves the board game community, but was surprised by "...the number of small to mid-weight publishers who work as a one person team from a living room or garage. We undervalue our indie creator community."[44]

Two years into working in the industry, Jesse makes enough to get by through his Patreon, YouTube ads, and some commercial video work. He plans to keep growing his channel, expand to a second channel, and give back even more to the community.

Notice that I didn't mention anything about money from the reviews themselves. He does this all for free for other creators. Some board game media companies charge for reviews or previews, and others do these for free. It's all a matter of what you feel is best for you and how you will make a living off of this endeavor if it is your main source of income. However, you do really need to have somewhat of a following before creators will be willing to part with their money.

Jesse admits that what he does takes a lot of work and that you have to outwork all the others who are trying to do the same thing as you. However, if you are committed and are willing to learn and go through all the growing pains that come with this, the potential is there.

When I asked Jesse what advice he would give to someone wanting to start their career in the board game industry, he simply said, "Work harder and care more."[44]

Just Pick Up a Camera and Hit "Record"

I also reached out to Richard Ham, aka Rahdo, who runs one of the most reputable board game review channels in the world, Rahdo Runs Through.

When I asked him how he got started doing board game reviews, like many others, he said he simply picked up a camera and went with it. He feels that anyone with their own camera can do what he does. It's all about finding your own niche and doing this in a way that is different from others out there.

Before he started his channel, Richard was a video game design lead. He had to be a cheerleader, leading his team, conveying his enthusiasm, and connecting with others. In his earlier years, he did telephone surveys and worked as a Nintendo game counselor, both of which involved a lot of communication, connection, and helping others.

He brings that cheerleading, charismatic character to his channel. It is a lot of work to put out multiple videos a week, over two hundred per year, but for Richard, it's all about quantity. People know they can go to his channel and find a whole lot of content on a ton of different games.

If a publisher sends him a game that he has discussed with them and has agreed to review, he feels obligated to cover it. However, if he receives a game that he doesn't enjoy, he gives the publisher the option if they want him to go ahead with the video, knowing it may do more harm than good.

One of the secrets of his prolific release schedule is that Richard does very little editing. He just lets the camera roll with little preparation so that he can run through a lot of games and keep providing lots of content. It also helps that he developed strong time management skills in his previous roles. Richard's background and experience being a cheerleader and enthusiastic person also comes through on his channel and people genuinely connect with him.

Richard never thought he'd be as popular as he has become. He was just hoping he would get lots of games to feed his gaming habit and didn't expect he'd be able to make a living at it. This was his biggest surprise. He imagined he'd do well and find an audience, but he never thought his channel would be one of the top five in the board game media world. The one thing he's not surprised by is the negativity he hears online, as he witnessed this in the video game industry prior. Getting pushback and unsubscribes from people for supporting Black Lives Matter is just one example of what he's had to experience. Not everyone will like your channel or agree with your opinions, so you have to be OK with this. Those who are your true fans will always be there.

After one year of doing Rahdo Runs Through, he had some traction but wasn't that well known yet. He went to Essen Spiel around that time and reached out to as many publishers as he could, sharing quotes and praise he received from other publishers about his videos. About 30 percent responded and gave him a review copy.

He continued to grow and funded his channel through multiple methods. In his early years, Richard ran Kickstarter campaigns for a few years to get the funds to purchase copies of games from publishers. He also earned revenue from YouTube ads and his Patreon.

This was enough to get by for a while, but things changed when he had to move from Malta back to the US, where the cost of living was much higher. He was doing free Kickstarter preview games prior to this and was one of the only ones not charging for this service. He has since started to charge for these videos over the past couple of years to make enough money. Even so, he rarely takes time off for vacations. He spends fifty-two weeks a year running his channel.

Richard tries to maintain reviewer integrity by not becoming close friends with anyone in the industry, as he wants to stay unbiased. He says, "I don't really develop relationships with anybody in my industry, and I do think it actually makes sense to kind of keep the industry at arms' length so I can maintain some kind of reviewer integrity… but at the end of the day, I'm really anti-social, and withdrawn, and shy, and quiet."[45]

His suggestion if you want to become a reviewer or other type of content creator is to just pick up a camera and do it. As long as he has a camera, some games, and good lighting, he can do this from anywhere—and freely admits that you can, too!

More broadly, if you want to work in the board game industry, Richard suggests you make contacts with publishers and offer to do anything for them—working a convention booth, playtesting games, editing rules, etc. When their company grows and they are in a position to hire, you'll be at the top of their mind.

You can also offer to help publishers get their games on digital platforms like Tabletop Simulator and Tabletopia. Publishers can never playtest enough, so anything you can do to help them with this is always greatly appreciated. I'll talk more about this in the next chapter as well.

When asked about whether he recommends someone pursuing a career in the industry, he said "There are people who have been very, very successful. But you know what, Hollywood is a major industry, too, and there are people who are very successful there, but the vast majority of people are not. I would not recommend you go out to Hollywood and pursue your dream of being a big-screen movie star, because the odds are against you. Same is true if you want to pursue your dreams of being a board game superstar. The odds are against you."[45]

While you may not become a superstar, there is no barrier to entry if you want to make your own game or help others in the industry. So, as Mark, Brittany, Jesse, and Rahdo all say, if you want to review games, just pick up a camera! Then find your style and discover a way to review in a way nobody else does.

Now, let's take a peek at some other industry-related jobs you may have never even given a thought to (but might be a great match for you!).

15

Ancillary Jobs and Other Outside-the-Box Ideas

We've already covered a lot of different roles and opportunities available to you in the industry, but in this chapter, we're going to discuss a number of alternatives you may never have even considered.

Many of these opportunities are meant to support others already in the industry, while others look at ways you can incorporate games into your current job.

Board Game Merchandise

There are millions of people who love board games. Many of them are wildly passionate about the hobby and want to share their love of these games with everyone around them.

So, what better way to help them express that love than by outfitting them with clothes and knick-knacks that embody the hobby?

That's what Chris Cormier does. He runs Geeky Goodies, a website dedicated to the board game nerd in all of us. He sells T-shirts, long-sleeve shirts, hoodies, mugs, posters, stickers, and lots of other great goodies for board gamers and geeks of many fandoms at GeekyGoodies.com.

After spending several years doing logo design and communications packages for small businesses, he decided to take something on that allowed him to be more creative and that combined his love of graphic design and board games.

DOI: 10.1201/9781003334408-20

He uses social media to bring attention to his company and products, creating hashtags that get used quite regularly. A lot of his business comes from word of mouth and repeat customers, along with those looking for gear from partners he works with, including Dice Tower and Foxtrot Games.

Chris' advice for anyone looking to get into the industry? "Start local, join the game nights at your local board game café or store, attend gaming events locally, and participate online with some of gaming communities and groups. Put yourself out there. I bet you will be surprised by the warm welcome you will receive!"[46]

Katia Howatson is another creative type who has turned her passion for board games into art. She runs a small side business called Board Game Art Creations.

She creates and photographs images made completely out of board game components. She translated this into an amazing looking boardgame mosaic calendar, which achieved funding successfully on Kickstarter. Her campaign also included full-size wall prints and Wingspan-inspired coasters. They are very cool creations!

These two examples show that gamers love their games and want to show their passions off through merchandise. So, if you can get creative, you might be able to make something that they will absolutely love.

Events

Conventions, or "cons," as we affectionately call them in the board game world, are popular events that are held all over the world, but especially in North America. Beyond conventions, there are plenty of Protospiels and other game design events as well.

These can range from a small con with a few dozen people to huge events like GenCon and Essen Spiel, which draw in tens of thousands of people.

Literally, hundreds of events take place every year, and someone needs to organize each and every one.

David Bloomberg is one of those organizers. He's one of the founders of Breakout Con, a small- to medium-sized con that brings over fifteen hundred gamers together at one big event every year, where I first met him. He's also involved in Tabs Con, a quarterly gaming event, and the Niagara Board Game Weekend.

David says that to be successful in organizing and growing events like this, you need to be a good listener. You'll get a lot of great suggestions from participants to make your event even better, so it's important to listen to your fans. Understanding finances is also crucial to ensure your event covers all expenses. Otherwise, you won't be able to return the following year.

David does this for the love of the hobby, not financial gain. Running one annual or quarterly event is hardly going to replace a full-time job, but it can be rewarding.[47]

I've also personally had the experience of co-organizing a gaming event. After enjoying a great weekend at Protospiel Michigan, a number of Torontonian game designers, including myself, started talking about how funny it was that we all traveled out of the country for an event like this when the Toronto gaming and game design scene are quite strong. So, we decided to run our own event closer to home the following year. We called it Protospiel North.

Our first event was quite successful, drawing in about fifty game designers and playtesters. We budgeted well and covered all the costs while learning many things that will help us run even better future events, like making it inexpensive for playtesters to attend, and avoiding scheduling it when other events were happening. We plan to run this again in post-pandemic times.

While running events aren't necessarily a good career path on their own, they can get you deeper into the gaming community. Volunteering and helping out at such events may connect you with others you can work with in the future. At the very least, you'll meet some great people who might become lifelong friends.

Agent/Broker

An agent (or broker) is someone who takes your product and presents it to potential companies or publishers, with the intention of licensing it to them.

While this role is more common in the toy industry, there is an opportunity here in the board game world as well. The margins are generally slim, but if you have (or can make) a lot of connections in the board game industry and already travel to some of the big events, you could partner with other game designers who aren't able to or aren't interested in attending these events and pitching to publishers.

You'd need to get familiar with the games you are representing and be able to pitch and demo them effectively. You'd likely be the one to put together a sell sheet and a video as well, depending on what arrangements you make with other designers.

The typical fee for an agent in the toy industry can range from 30 to 60 percent of the royalties, but some may work on an upfront-payment model. As in most cases in this industry, the payout isn't huge and would come well in the future. You'd need to work on high volume, as well as select games with the most potential.

You also need to be sure you can cover your costs since attending conventions can get expensive. At the same time, if you have a good network of connections, you can also reach out to contacts directly and pitch games without needing to attend every event. This will definitely help to keep your expenses down.

Translations

Board games are played all over the world. Not everyone speaks English, so there is a demand to create rulebooks and other materials in the native languages in which games are sold.

Enter translators.

I've had and have taken up multiple offers to translate the rules for *Relics of Rajavihara* into other languages. The exchange has generally been a translation for a copy (or two or three) of the game.

This is a great way to add games you'd love to play to your collection, but not a great way to make a living! However, if you prove yourself as a great translator who is easy to work with, you can quickly build a portfolio. This, in turn, could be used to start your own side business where you connect with bigger publishers and negotiate for paid translations.

If you can prove your skills and build up a client base, this could turn into something even bigger for you, especially if you could build a team of translators and offer publishers a one-stop-shop for all their translation needs.

Crowdfunding

Here's another adjacent industry you may not have thought of: crowdfunding.

Pop quiz. Do you know what the number-one category for money raised on Kickstarter is? Games.

And what's the number-one subcategory within games? Tabletop games. By far.[48]

In fact, tabletop games earn more than ten times more than the next subcategory: video games. So, you could say that board games are a pretty big deal on Kickstarter![49]

While Kickstarter is the biggest crowdfunding site, others are out there, too, including Indiegogo and two newer sites dedicated strictly to board games: Game on Tabletop and Gamefound.

All these sites need people to run them. They need founders to create and manage them, programmers to set up the sites and allow them to make transactions, project managers to keep things running smoothly, and many, many others.

You can see how one industry can quickly spawn multiple related industries and companies.

Game creators (and many other creators for that matter) had gatekeepers and the barrier to entry was high, so Kickstarter came along to make it easier. This is another case of someone recognizing a gap and creating a service to fill it.

But what about sales after the campaign? That was beyond the initial scope of Kickstarter, so pledge managers came along. Now we have a variety of sites to handle this, including Gamefound, Crowdox, Backerkit, Pledge Manager, and others. Some people love to see statistics or what games are coming soon, so other sites like Kicktraq (which makes money through advertising other campaigns) and Bigger Cake filled that need.

Whenever you see a need that is not being filled, see it as an opportunity. Whether you have an interest in starting your own company or would prefer to join a new startup to take on these challenges, the prospects are there for the taking.

Playtesting and Digital Services

If there's one thing publishers (and smaller creators) can never get enough of, it is playtesting. In order to make a good game into an amazing game, it has to be playtested dozens or hundreds of times. Not everyone has the time or connections to do this.

Matt Holden realized this. That's why he started the Indie Game Alliance (IGA). It's a resource for publishers, designers, and others in the profession that connects publishers with playtesters who actually want to play your game.

Here's how it works: Publishers send copies of their game or prototype to IGA. Volunteers (known as "minions") select games they'd like to playtest. The game is shipped to the playtester, who plays it with their gaming group and gathers valuable feedback for the publisher, in exchange for credits that can be exchanged for copies of games they would like to own.[50]

It's a win-win proposition.

There are very few organizations that offer playtesting services, so at the moment it is an underserved need. Whether it is a model similar to what IGA offers or a professional service you could run on your own, the opportunity is there.

IGA also demos and sells games at conventions and partners with others in the industry to offer paying members discounts on everything from manufacturing to digital adaptations of games.

Speaking of digital adaptations, many publishers and designers are either not tech savvy or are too busy to have the time to port their games over to digital platforms. If you take the time to learn platforms like Tabletop Simulator (TTS) or Tabletopia, you will have an in-demand skill that can support these publishers—even more so if you can learn scripting on TTS.

If you're good with programs like Blendr or others, you could create mods (essentially files) with cool components creators would love. Share some free stuff and get active on social media and you could soon have people asking if they can pay you to create custom components for their games.

There are a few individuals out there offering this service, including Timothy Metcalfe, whom I have hired to do some light scripting and bug fixes that were beyond my level of TTS expertise.

Imagine being able to offer publishers a way to get even more people's eyes on their game. That sounds like a service they would be willing to pay for.

Then there's Board Game Arena, a site dedicated to the digital implementation of hundreds of games. While they typically use volunteers to code games, the individuals running it have struck upon a very popular platform.

Think Outside the Box

Print and Play (PnP) games are becoming more and more popular. These are games that you can download as a PDF and put together on your own, often adding common components like dice and pawns, to give you everything you need to play. People often like to try before they buy, while others simply enjoy crafting their own version of a game.

While this is definitely a niche within a niche and many people don't want to take the time and effort to build a Print and Play game, there is an audience for them. Some people will even back the PnP level of a Kickstarter campaign for a small cost.

PnP Arcade (pnparcade.com) offers Print and Play games for just a few dollars and even has some games available for free. It's a one-stop shop for PnP games.

Not all creators are good at making PnP versions of their games though. There's a lot to think about in order to make it as easy as possible for players to prepare everything and get it to the table quickly. Games that are too complicated to figure out or don't print correctly will end up just sitting on their hard drive.

Is there an opportunity to provide a service that would create PnP versions of games? *I* don't know, but your mind might be whirring at the concept.

What gaps have you noticed in the board game industry? What opportunities are out there? What are you good at that people would pay you for, so they don't have to do a task they're not good at or don't enjoy?

Always be asking these kinds of questions. Always be thinking about what you can do for others to help them succeed, and before long, you'll find your opportunity.

16

Making Games Part of Your Own Job

Transitioning from your current career into a field that generally pays less and can be much less stable is not for everyone. If you have mouths to feed and bills to pay, it could be irresponsible to throw everything away and pursue a crazy dream like this, at least for right now (though remember, you can always do this on the side!).

If the thought of leaving your day job or running your own business scares you, there is something else you might want to consider: what if you could make gaming part of your existing job?

Now, while I admit this won't work for everyone or every industry, there may be ways to bring games or game-based learning into your current role. This is especially the case if your job involves training or teaching in some way.

Teaching Game Design

Kathleen Mercury is a schoolteacher. She works with gifted children and has a fair amount of autonomy, so long as she covers the curriculum and supports the needs of her students. She was a guest in my Board Game Design Virtual Summit 2020 and she was a pleasure to talk to.

Kathleen began teaching game design to her students when she discovered that it could teach them a lot about problem-solving, working collaboratively, giving constructive feedback, and that failure is part of life (and it's

DOI: 10.1201/9781003334408-21

also a great teacher!). Before long, her students were creating games all on their own.

As Kathleen explains, "I began teaching game design to my students, and I began designing games with them. Designing games with them forced me to persist and keep going along with them, and I discovered I really loved the process. I'm a really outgoing person and I love to learn, so whenever I met a designer, I was just so curious about their process. I would ask so many questions, both to improve my classes as well as to improve my own designs. With a bit of moxie and support from my friends, I began showing my games to publishers."[51]

Some of those games have now been signed with these same publishers.

In addition to teaching game design and designing her own games, she co-hosts the Board Game Broads podcast and runs the website www.kathleenmercury.com, which hosts game design resources that are used at all levels and around the world.[51]

I've had my own experiences teaching game design as well. I was hired (on a one-term contract position, covering for a leave) to teach first-year students at Laurier University in their Game Design and Development program, and now I run two of my own online game design courses. I've also volunteered in multiple classrooms teaching students about game design and assisting teachers by developing games to teach topics like pulleys and gears, light and sound, and the rock formation cycle (who knew you could make a topic like that fun?). If you have the skills and experience, you can always help others who aren't as far along or well-versed as you.

My wife, who is a teacher, has also incorporated games into some of her lessons. She has taught anywhere from Kindergarten to Grade 3 over the past decade and finds that games are a compelling way to teach many subjects and key learning skills. She's used games like *Forbidden Island* to teach cooperation, dice games like my own *I Scream For Dice Cream* to teach probability and math, and games like *Tsuro* to help students recognize patterns and think strategically.

If you teach, do corporate consulting, or something similar, there are plenty of ways you can use games and game-based learning with your students or clients. These can range from ice-breakers to problem-solving games and activities where group members have to work together to build a structure, figure out how to survive a plane crash, or re-imagine an assembly process.

Let's look at one more example before we wrap this up.

Board Gaming with Education

Dustin Staats runs Board Gaming with Education with his wife. It started out as a podcast, but they quickly branched into selling games to educators, homeschool parents, and families. They also provide courses, professional development, and consulting.

Dustin has had to not only find his niche but also create this niche on his own. Board games are sometimes used in classrooms to help to teach the curriculum, but this is not yet a mainstream concept. After running their business on the side for three years while working a full-time job, he is now transitioning to doing this full-time.

Like many others, Dustin suggests volunteering as a first step to getting into the industry. Find a way to lend a hand and help others. That way, you'll get to see what the industry is like firsthand and decide if it is right for you.

However, if you're ready to take the plunge and start your own business within the board game industry, he suggests you just start. Don't wait for the perfect tools, business name, timing, or anything else. You'll hold yourself back and delay moving forward until everything is perfect, and there will always be something that isn't perfect. Take a "done is better than perfect" mantra and get working!

When I asked Dustin whether he would recommend changing careers to join the board game industry, he shared a resounding "Yes! Only if you are comfortable turning your passion into your work. Not everyone likes to have their passions and work overlap, and I would suggest dipping your toes in first and seeing if it is for you."[52]

Yet again, we see the safe approach suggested. Rather than jumping in with both feet before you know what you're getting into, take advantage of one of the many opportunities outlined throughout this book. Then determine if this is the right fit for you, build your way up, and see where your dreams and hard work can take you!

17

Conclusion

While there are a lot of job opportunities in the board game industry and some obvious gaps that are just waiting for the right people to fill them, there are many common discoveries we've made about working in the industry throughout this book.

The pay generally isn't great. People aren't in the board game industry to make a quick buck or strike it rich. They are in it because they love board games, enjoy the creativity and flexibility that often comes with the job, and value these things above money. If you're looking for easy money, this probably isn't the place for you.

You need to have good interpersonal skills. Board games, by nature, are highly social. Working in the industry is no different. You need to be able to communicate effectively and be able to listen to and work with others. You must be able to clearly articulate what you want out of a project, explain what you bring to a project, and understand what others want to get out of a project.

You need to be a good problem-solver. Whether you are developing a game, working as a publisher, are involved in shipping and fulfillment, providing art or graphic design services, creating content, or anything else, you constantly need to get to the root of an issue and find viable solutions. Game designers are constantly solving problems (and often adding new ones when we fix others), but this thread is common throughout the industry, not just in design.

You need to be motivated and have a great work ethic. It goes without saying that being a hard worker is important. You need to constantly be learning, improving, and getting better in your role. You need to be curious. And you need to be willing to put in the time and effort to build a portfolio, a reputation, and gain the trust of others. Many roles in the industry are freelance or otherwise fairly independent, and you need to be able to deliver results.

Because the industry doesn't have a ton of full-time positions, you'll often have to work part-time or as a freelancer. Almost everyone I connected with said that it is best to get into the industry by doing this on the side, through volunteering, discovering what you enjoy and are good at, and building your portfolio before considering jumping into this full-time.

This is especially the case if you are the breadwinner of the family and/or need to earn a decent wage to get by. If you're in the fortunate situation of having a partner who can support you financially (as well as in other ways) or have some savings and little to no debt, it can certainly make the transition easier. Living more frugally or in a region that has a lower cost of living can also help.

So, if you're still thinking about a career in the board game industry and I haven't scared you off yet, I recommend starting off by doing something you love, on the side. That way you'll find out if it's something that you'll want to keep doing long term. You may even discover something related to this or meet someone who is looking for someone with your skills for an upcoming project.

Be consistent, help others, and work your way up. Don't be afraid to do some free or underpaid work just to get started and build your portfolio, along with your reputation. Many others who contributed to this book did exactly that before they became more well-known. Once people see what you're capable of, you'll be able to earn what your skills are worth.

Recognize that opportunities are out there if you have the right skills, are willing to work hard, and money is not as important to you as creativity, flexibility, and doing what you love.

You'll notice that many of the roles discussed in this book have no specific educational requirements. Roles like graphic design and artwork, positions that highly rely on special schooling, and roles related to marketing and project management definitely benefit from the right educational backgrounds, but most other positions are self-taught. You can learn a lot through on-the-job experience, and the more experience you get, the better you will be in that role. You can show companies that you are indispensable.

It's all about matching your skills to the positions out there, making a name for yourself in the industry by meeting others and demonstrating those skills, and discovering and filling those important gaps you see.

I hope you've found this book helpful and that you find your place in a role that only you can fill in this amazing industry.

Now, if you're ready to find your niche in the board game world, get out there and show everyone how you can make it an even better place. There's no reason to roll the dice and hope for a great outcome. Instead, find your place, test the waters, and build up your reputation and portfolio. There's a role out there that only you can fill.

Suggested Resources

Looking for more info on board game design and the industry at large? Check out these great books, blogs, and podcasts.

Books

Barrett, Gabe. *Board Game Design Advice: From the Best in the World*. Barrett Publishing, 2018.

Barrett, Gabe. *Board Game Kickstarter Advice: From the Best in the World*. Barrett Publishing, 2020.

Garfield, Richard and Steve Jackson. *Kobold Guide to Board Game Design*. Open Design LLC, 2011.

Koster, Raph. *Theory of Fun for Game Design*. O'Reilly Media, 2013.

Schell, Jesse. *The Art of Game Design: A Book of Lenses*. CRC Press, 2017.

Slack, Joe. *The Board Game Designer's Guide*. 2017.

Slack, Joe. *The Board Game Designer's Guide to Getting Published*. 2020.

Slack, Joe. *The Top 10 Mistakes New Board Game Designers Make (and How to Avoid Them)*. 2020.

Stegmaier, Jamey. *A Crowdfunder's Strategy Guide: Build a Better Business by Building Community*. Berrett-Koehler Publishers, 2015.

Tinsman, Brian, et al. *The Game Inventor's Guidebook*. Morgan James Publishing, 2008.

Blogs, Podcasts, and Websites

- Board Game Design Lab—an excellent resource for information and my personal favorite podcast on game design:
  http://www.boardgamedesignlab.com/
- Boardgamegeek—the most comprehensive resource for all things board game-related:
  www.boardgamegeek.com
- Cardboard Edison—website and Compendium, a great source listing hundreds of publishers:
  http://cardboardedison.com/
  http://cardboardedison.com/directoryinfo/

- Indie Game Alliance—a helpful organization that provides discounts on board game-related services: https://www.indiegamealliance.com/
- Kickstarter Lessons and Amazing Self-publishing and Board Game Design Tips from Jamey Stegmaier of Stonemaier Games: https://stonemaiergames.com/kickstarter/how-to-design-a-tabletop-game/
- Ludology—a great podcast about the "why" of game design http://ludology.libsyn.com/

Endnotes

1. John Zinser, in discussion with the author. December 2020.
2. Sen-Foong Lim, in discussion with the author. December 2020.
3. Jason Schneider, in discussion with the author. December 2020.
4. Justin De Witt, in discussion with the author. December 2020.
5. Curt Covert, in discussion with the author. December 2020.
6. Adam McCrimmon, in discussion with the author. December 2020.
7. Scott Gaeta, in discussion with the author. December 2020.
8. Scott Gaeta, "How to Turn Your Gaming Passion into a Gaming Career with Scott Gaeta", Proto TO, Dec 3, 2017, https://www.youtube.com/watch?v=nfcI-MTpxfo.
9. Fertessa Allyse, in discussion with the author. December 2020.
10. John-Baptiste Ramassamy, in discussion with the author. December 2020.
11. Joshua Lobkowicz, in discussion with the author. December 2020.
12. Sydney Engelstein, in discussion with the author. December 2020.
13. Debbie Moynihan, in discussion with the author. December 2020.
14. Patrick Marino, in discussion with the author. December 2020.
15. Joe Aubrey, in discussion with the author. December 2020.
16. Alexander Schmidt, in discussion with the author. December 2020.
17. Rachael Blaske, in discussion with the author. January 2021.
18. Anne-Marie De Witt, in discussion with the author. December 2020.
19. Jamey Stegmaier, in discussion with the author. December 2020.
20. Vincent Vergonjeanne, in discussion with the author. December 2020.
21. Sebastian Koziner, in discussion with the author. December 2020.
22. Matt Paquette, in discussion with the author. December 2020.
23. Hanna Björkman, in discussion with the author. December 2020.
24. Tristam Rossin, in discussion with the author. January 2021.
25. Beth Sobel, In Focus - Interview with Beth Sobel, Punchboard Media, July 5, 2017, https://www.punchboardmedia.com/home/2017/7/5/punchboard-media-in-focus-interview-with-beth-sobel. Accessed January 2021.
26. Kwanchai Moriya, https://www.kwanchaimoriya.com/. Accessed January 2021.
27. Vincent Dutrait, Vincent Dutrait – master of board game art, Greenhook Games, June 26, 2016, http://www.greenhookgames.com/vincent-dutrait/. Accessed January 2021.
28. Nikki Valens, In Focus - Interview with Nikki Valens, Punchboard Media, June 6, 2018, https://www.punchboardmedia.com/home/2018/6/6/punchboard-media-in-focus-interview-with-nikki-valens. Accessed January 2021.
29. Dustin Schwartz, https://therulesforge.com/. Accessed January 2021.
30. Jeff Fraser, in discussion with the author. December 2020.
31. Shero Li, in discussion with the author. December 2020.
32. Kerry Rundle and Sarah Graybill, in discussion with the author. August 2020.
33. Dave Snyder, in discussion with the author. December 2020.

34. Jon Homfray, in discussion with the author. January 2021

35. Tyler Smith, in discussion with the author. January 2021.

36. AJ Brandon, in discussion with the author. December 2020.

37. Nalin Chuapetcharasopon, in discussion with the author. December 2020.

38. Brandon Rollins, in discussion with the author. January 2021.

39. Ori Kagan, in discussion with the author. December 2020.

40. David Diaz, in discussion with the author. December 2020.

41. Gabe Barrett, in discussion with the author. January 2021.

42. Cameron Art, in discussion with the author. December 2020.

43. Mark Maia, in discussion with the author. January 2021.

44. Jesse Samuel Anderson, in discussion with the author. January 2021.

45. Richard Ham, in discussion with the author. December 2020.

46. Chris Cormier, in discussion with the author. December 2020.

47. David Bloomberg, in discussion with the author. December 2020.

48. Kickstarter, Kickstarter Stats, https://www.kickstarter.com/help/stats. Accessed February 2021.

49. ICO Partners, Kickstarter and Games in 2019, January 2020, https://icopartners.com/2020/01/kickstarter-and-games-in-2019/. Accessed February 2021.

50. Indie Game Alliance, https://indiegamealliance.com/. Accessed February 2021.

51. Kathleen Mercury, in discussion with the author. January 2021.

52. Dustin Staats, in discussion with the author. December 2020.

Thank You!

Thank you so much for reading my book! There are tons of game design resources out there, so I'm very appreciative that you chose mine.

I'd really love to have your feedback and to know how my book was beneficial to you.

Help me spread the word so other future industry professionals can also benefit from this book.

Thanks so much!

~Joe Slack